EIGHT REASONS FOR CRIME

Introducing a Sociological Perspective

MARLEY HILL

Copyright © 2022 Inkerbook Press

All rights reserved. This book or any portion thereof may not be reproduced or used in any manner whatsoever without the express written permission of the publisher except for the use of brief quotations in a book review.

ISBN: 9798487145154

Printed by Inkerbook Press, in the United States of America

Inkerbook Press
Alexandra
New Zealand

Email: info@inkrebook.com
www.inkerbook.com

CONTENTS

Introduction 1

Chapter 1 – Criminals And Victims 5

Chapter 2 – The Upbringing 17

Chapter 3 – Money Talks 27

Chapter 4 – Uppers and Downers 37

Chapter 5 – It's Who You Know 49

Chapter 6 – It's All Political 61

Chapter 7 – As God Is My Witness 73

Chapter 8 – Time Isn't On My Side 85

Chapter 9 – Liberty And Justice For All 97

Chapter 10 – Crime And Punishment 109

Conclusion 119

About The Author 123

References 125

INTRODUCTION

We know crime exists. Look at any front page of the newspaper, or on a news internet site, or listen to the top three stories on the evening news bulletins. Odds are, at least one of them will be a story about a crime. "If it bleeds, it leads," is a fairly common mantra among those in charge of these sites. It seems to be part of our nature to follow these stories avidly. Who has more name recognition—the person who committed the crime or the victims of it? Unfortunately, although we might care for the victim, we are more likely to know who the criminal is. What we don't always know is why. We speculate, but our knowledge is either hampered by not knowing the circumstances behind the crime or by our lack of understanding of the relationship between victim and perpetrator. Why did an apparently loving mother kill her son? What led the man to commit the rape? Is there any justification for the armed holdup that ended so badly? It's likely that unless we serve on the jury or are intimately involved in the crime through personal knowledge of the criminal or victim, that we will never have any more insight than what we see or hear on news sites. So, we are left to guess.

Crime is, by its very nature, something that we never want to experience. There is a lot written about "victimless" crime, but is there really any such thing? Somewhere, someone always pays, whether it's faceless insurance companies who are ripped off by a con artist or the government that is forced to fix the situation when a government official goes rogue. But most crimes involve more than just those who committed the crime and those who suffered from it. Criminals are not usually born—they become criminals thanks to other issues in their lives. And that is what we are going to have a look at in this book. We love pictures of newborn babies, but how many of us look at the picture of the baby and think—that kid has "murderer" written all over his face.

It is easy to dismiss the criminal as someone who deserves their fate. Take a look at the comments section of a story reporting on the details of a crime. The more gory or repugnant the better. Somewhere in the comments is bound to be something along the lines of "hang the bastard" or "no sympathy—hope he gets raped in prison."

We don't have to feel sympathy for the criminal. But it would be helpful to understand why they did what they did. We can't change what happened, but we can as a society learn from it. "Those who fail to learn from history are condemned to repeat it" is a quote attributed to Winston Churchill in a speech to the House of Commons in 1948. He was not referring to crime in this speech, more about world events, but it's as good a theory as any when it comes to considering how even the most tragic of situations can have the smallest of silver linings.

As far as what causes crime, if only we knew for sure! We could stop all crime RIGHT NOW!

But we can't do that. Crime is complex, and the motives behind the crime are not as simple as saying that a criminal is a bad person. End of.

So that's what I'm going to try to do in this book. Explore what turns that new, innocent baby into a criminal who hurts others by acts that we don't understand. We are going to look at what we commonly think of as causes of crimes and why we need to fix the problem at the source. We will never eliminate crime—that is a Utopian concept. What we can do is at least try to stop conditions that lead to the person committing the act in the first place. This isn't a magic bullet that will solve crime. But if we can reduce crime and its effect on us, then that can only be an improvement. Let's start by looking at what crime is, who the criminals are, and who they affect.

CHAPTER 1
CRIMINALS AND VICTIMS

"Neither the passions nor justice nor politics nor the great social forces ever consider the victims they strike." ~ Honore De Balzac

Crime. It's everywhere. From minor crimes to the most horrific, we see and hear about at least one crime being committed every day. No city is immune, and no country has an armlock on a nil-crime day. We all know someone who knows someone who has been a victim of crime (if, in fact, we ourselves are not the victim).

Less common is knowing a criminal. (Or if we do know a criminal, not realizing that they are one.) There doesn't tend to be a one-to-one crime: criminal ratio. For example, two people could rob a home. The odds are this home had more or less than two people living there, so the people directly affected by the robbery do not equal those who committed the robbery. Murderers are known to work in pairs, or groups, to kill more than one person at a time or over time.

The crime: criminal ratio is further expanded when you consider those who are indirectly affected. The murderer kills a victim, so clearly, the victim is the person primarily affected. But few victims live in vacuums, and those who survive or who were close to the victim are secondarily affected. A rapist may rape one person, but those close to that person (particularly a spouse or significant other) are also victims of that rape. The effect of the crime multiplies the number of victims; hence why we all know of a victim, but few of us know of a perp.

It's hard to understand crime without understanding the criminal. What makes someone decide to go outside the law? In the next chapters, we'll go through some possible reasons why people do, but first, let's look at the typical criminal.

For starters, the criminal is probably male. Women are starting to close this gender gap, but overwhelmingly, crime is a male prerogative. Statistics from the United States Department of Justice[1] show that in 2019, arrests from reported offenses of all types were 10,085,210. Of these, 7,316,520 arrests were of males.

Crime is still a younger person's game. While the US Federal Bureau of Investigation information shows that children and the over 60s have been arrested and charged with all types of crime, including murder and manslaughter, the bulk of criminal offending occurs[2] in the three age groups 25-29, 30-34, and 35-39. These groups commit 17%, 13%, and 10%, respectively, of all crimes.

The majority of violent crimes occur in Central and South American countries[3]. Los Cabos, Mexico, sees more murders per 100,000 head of population than any other city in the world. The other cities in the top five are Caracas (Venezuela), Acapulco (Mexico), Natal (Brazil), and Tijuana (Mexico).

Property crime is the most common offense. This includes burglary, motor vehicle-related thefts, and arson. After property crime, the next most common is driving under the influence of alcohol or drugs. Drug-related offenses are the use, possession, manufacturing, and distribution of illegal substances and are the next most commonly reported crimes. Even though it's a crime we hear most about, murder is not a particularly common offense. Perhaps it's murder's rarity that makes it the reportable one — remember that if it bleeds, it leads, and bad news sells.

The issue of race and its link to crime will be addressed in a later chapter. For now, we are only looking at the portrait of a criminal, not the whys. And the portrait shows that when taking into account the per head of population in each racial group, the majority of those arrested for crimes are non-Caucasian.

When it comes to murder, while we hear plenty about murders committed against close family members, it's statistically more likely that the murderer has a nodding acquaintance at best with the victim. This includes school shootings and acts of terrorism, where the victim count is more important than who is murdered. However, when we look at crimes of violence that lead to murder, these are most commonly a more intimate affair. A female is statistically more likely to be assaulted or murdered by a partner or husband than she is by a total stranger.

Rape is a crime that is widely acknowledged to be under-reported, so there are no accurate statistics on who commits rape and who the victim is. This is complicated by the evidence that suggests that stranger-rape cases are far more likely to result in a conviction, whether this is because the victim is more readily believed in a stranger case or because the "he-said-she-said" mantra doesn't come up as often in stranger rapes. Consent, in other words, is more likely to be an issue in acquaintance rape. RAINN statistics show, however, that of reported rapes, in most cases, the victim knows the perpetrator[4].

Gang-related offenses are across the board. Let's be clear – not all gang members are criminals, and we should never assume that just because someone is a member of a gang, that they have been lured in by the prospect of criminal behavior. However, gang criminal activities range from minor larceny to drug deals to all-out murder. Violence between gangs over territory is commonplace.

So the average person who is convicted of a criminal act is youngish, male, and probably Black or another ethnic minority. Depending on the nature of his offense, he may or may not know his victim, and while it's not a given, he is probably a gang member.

As for his victim? It's probably his spouse, girlfriend, gang enemy, or drug dealer. Or a total stranger. In other words, anyone.

We are all potential victims of crime. We may be more vulnerable to certain types of crime, such as family or intimate violence, or because we are active gang members. We could be addicts, specifically drug addicts (again, there will be a more in-depth discussion on the links between addiction and crime in a later chapter).

Whether we commit crimes might actually have more to do with geography than circumstance. In some countries or states, prostitution is legal. Others, not, so those of us who practice prostitution as a profession are criminals in some parts of the world. Other examples of activities that are criminal in one area and not in others are drug possession, blasphemy, and homosexuality.

If we commit crimes or are victims of crimes, what are the odds that we will be brought to justice or have justice served? As mentioned, the most common crime that slips under the radar is rape, particularly date or acquaintance rape. The chances of conviction are low, and those who claim that they were raped are often not keen to come forward to face their accuser or even to submit to the intrusive physical examination required. Shame and fear are other reasons that rape is an under-reported crime. While we tend to think of women as the victims of rapes, men get raped too, both by other men and by women, and the indications are that these men are even less likely to come forward. We also tend to think of the women who are raped as being young, but again, there is no age limit.

We need to acknowledge that there is a difference between crimes that get reported versus crimes that get convicted. Even though murder is not the most common of crimes, it is (and be thankful for this!) the crime where there is most often a conviction. There are cases where the police get it wrong, and there are cases where murderers walk, for whatever reason—a poor case, insufficient evidence, or in the worst cases, a corrupt system—but in the main, the person who is arrested for the crime is more often than not the person who is convicted of the crime. And rightly so. murder is the extreme of crimes, these are the cases that we remember. They play out on the news every night of the court case. We know more about the criminal than we do the victim. When there is a component that makes the crime into clickbait, like a particularly horrendous murder, such as that of a child, or a serial killer, the news is played out across the internet, news stations, and social media. We know the killer's name, his (as we said before, it's mostly a "he") face, and where he grew up. His victims are remembered, but they are less well-known. We have an emotional connection with his victim—he or she (or they) could be our kids, sisters, friends. But they are dead, and our connection with them is loose at best. However, the more emotional we feel toward those who have died, the angrier we feel about those who killed them. "I'd like to string him up" or "put him in a room alone with me for five minutes" are phrases that often crop up (thank you social media or comments section) when the criminal's face shows up on the news. And that, naturally, brings on even more vitriol, more commentary. And that brings on more clicks. It's all about the clicks.

But in reality, the most common punishment for crime is probation. That is because the most common crimes are at the lower end of the scale. Rehabilitation is considered more important than punishment for crimes that, while they certainly hurt people, don't necessarily destroy them. If you have ever been burgled, you will have lost possessions dear to you. You may not have insurance, meaning that the criminal has taken more than just a computer or a piece of jewelry—they have made it difficult for you to replace that. And even if you do have insurance, no one really likes dealing with insurance claims! Then there's the sense of personal grievance—that violation because a (presumed) total stranger has been in your home. Your feeling of safety and security is gone. But you are alive, your family is alive, and no one is damaged irreparably. The person who did this to you is, and should, be given a chance to learn from what they did, rather than be punished for it. So probation it is.

As the degree of crime intensifies, so too do the sentences. The United States operates under a felony system – the greater the felony, the longer or more punishing the sentence. There are felony misdemeanors, such as traffic offenses, failing to stop when requested by police, or possession of an illegal weapon. Most of these will see the perpetrator theoretically incur a year's imprisonment. (Theoretically, as judges impose sentences and have the discretion to lengthen or shorten the sentence if they feel it appropriate). Burglary may not be considered a serious offense, but add a weapon into the mix, and suddenly, what was previously considered a minor offense is taken to another level (and understandably so). When we have been burgled, and we are unharmed, that is one thing. If we were burgled and threatened, the damage is less to our property than to our safety and security.

Who the victim is, also carries weight with the sentencing judge. If we are vulnerable, such as a child or an older person, the judge is likely to look less fondly on the person who that crime. Someone convicted of the rape of an adult may or may not get a long sentence. convicted of the rape of a child will almost certainly spend several years behind bars.

Crimes committed in the course of committing other crimes also incur the multiplier effect. Hence, assault with a deadly weapon will earn the criminal a harsher sentence than one where the crime involves a less likely threat. Someone who injures another while driving a vehicle will incur a lighter sentence than if that person was driving under the influence of drugs or alcohol.

Naturally, the harshest penalties—death or life imprisonment—are reserved for those crimes that affect the victims the most. Murder, extremely aggravated assault, and terrorism are crimes where the perpetrator is likely to spend the rest of their lives in prison. Drug trafficking is punishable by death in several countries, particularly in Asia. The United States is ununited when it comes to the death penalty—the likelihood of being executed for murder in the USA is very much dependent on geography. If you murder another person in Texas, your chances of being executed are high. If you were to step across the New Mexico border to kill someone, your chances of being executed are nil.

Life imprisonment doesn't necessarily mean life behind bars, either. In some countries, such as Canada, a life sentence can be as short as seven years before the criminal can apply for parole. In other countries, life means a minimum of ten years, others it is 25. The nature of the sentence is usually not up for debate; the length is, however. This is where judges have the discretion to impose longer sentences for murder or crimes of violence where the crime is particularly heinous, such as child murder, or multiple murders, or murders committed against a particular group (cop killers will almost certainly get a harsher sentence in the USA than someone who killed a civilian). And parole tends not to be a given; few murderers go to prison, stick it out for the 10–15-year minimum non-parole period, and then automatically walk out.

We are becoming both tougher and more lenient on crime and criminals. As a general rule, we do not send people to prison to punish them. Rehabilitation is considered a far more practical method of redemption than harsher penalties. We invest in rehab programs for less violent crimes because, frankly, this makes more sense. We don't want criminals to go to prison – we would far prefer them not to commit crimes in the first place. But having committed an offense that society deems to be unacceptable, we would instead prefer that the criminal never committed such an offense again. And this is where rehabilitation is much more effective than retribution. There is no point in sending a criminal to prison, where they will likely be exposed to more violent offenders, with no chance of changing their behavior and having them walk out at the end of their sentence as reformed characters. Nevertheless, statistics indicate[5] that recidivist offenders make up more than 60% of those who are imprisoned every year.

But one form of sentencing that has been trialed, and not always to good effect, is the "three strikes" rule. This is a law that mandates a life prison sentence when the criminal has committed two prior offenses, one of which may be a drug offense or a crime of violence. How the three-strike rule is applied varies. In the United States, initially, the three strikes could be any three crimes, including what would otherwise be described as misdemeanors. Amendments to the rules have taken away some of the absurdities of the system, for example, life sentences imposed for petty theft, because the offender had committed two petty thefts already. Additionally, some states allowed the three-strike rules to apply to crimes committed by juveniles. The sentencing judge will now often have discretion (initially, there was no discretion — judges had no choice as to what sentence to impose under the three-strike rule).

So what options do we have if the prison sentence doesn't work? Are murderers put off by the likelihood that they will be executed if caught? Do rapists consider that a few years behind bars is a small price to pay for forcible sexual connection? Drug smugglers may well be executed if caught, but clearly, they are not all caught, and the rewards are high, so many are ready to take the risk. Those who commit lesser crimes are not going to be dissuaded by the thought of probation – the risk-reward ratio here definitely favors those who grab that particular brass ring.

We can try. We invest in sex offender programs in prison to reduce the chances that the child molester stops. We encourage drug and alcohol programs to help those who have addiction issues that, if left untreated, will probably lead the person back into crime when they leave. We offer education assistance and work-release programs to hopefully give the criminal valuable coping tools for when they are released. In some countries and regions, we have the option of the "clean slate," where someone who has committed a relatively minor crime can have their record "wiped clean" as though the crime was never committed. This has special significance in cases where a criminal record prevents the offender from obtaining employment or other benefits, like housing. And in the worst-case scenarios, we can and do keep the most heinous offenders in prison indefinitely. This is intended as punishment but also as protection. For the criminal, who, if released, could be a target for vigilantes, but more importantly, for the public.

But we cannot escape crime. We have yet to figure out how to build a Utopian society where all citizens are safe and healthy, where no criminals walk among us. All we can do is to look at what crimes occur and why, and see if there is any way we can reduce the chances of someone walking down that path. And it starts when we are young. Let's take a look at the early life of criminals.

CHAPTER 2

THE UPBRINGING

"Give me a child until he is 7, and I will show you the man." ~ Aristotle

Our family is the most intense school we will ever attend. We are born into it (or adopted into it), and it shapes our lives. We look to our parents, or parental units, as our first teachers. No child is born speaking or even walking. Our only innate traits are that of sucking and some hand and body movements. Even smiling is something we pick up from others. So it's understandable that how we are raised plays a major part in how we live our lives.

Where we are raised also helps determine how we will live. Some children are dealt an unlucky hand when it comes to the environment. As we noted in Chapter one, the most dangerous countries in the world when it comes to violent crimes are Mexico, Brazil, and Venezuela. If we are born in those countries, we are more likely to be born into an environment where we are exposed to violence and, therefore, we are more likely to be attuned to it. As we grow up, it is probably inevitable that we either accept it as a way of life or even begin to participate in violent acts. Or we attempt to escape from it by leaving the country of our birth, thus, losing our ties to our family and community. And when we get to our new country, we might struggle to fit in, especially if we are in the new country illegally (so are criminals almost from the moment we step inside that country's border). As illegals, our job prospects are limited, as are our chances of finding good housing. We have brought our family into a "better' country, but that doesn't mean we can give them a safer or better life.

Some countries have been at war for many years, particularly in the Middle East. Children raised in those countries are more likely to see bombed schools than functioning classrooms. Their parents may have been killed or maimed by airstrikes, leaving their children exposed to the dangers of being raised without support or what people in other countries would consider to be a normal, healthy home life. They miss out on the chance for education, and are exposed to dangers other children, who got lucky when they were born in a safer country, can never understand.

Then there's the divide between those children born in wealthy countries and those whose daily existence is one of starvation or, at the very least, deprivation. Children are born into poverty in every country in the world, but to paraphrase George Orwell in Animal Farm, "all countries are equally poor, but some are less poor than others." There is poverty, and then there is desperate poverty. Some countries are in a position to help their poorer citizens, and then there are countries where the resources just aren't available. A child born in a wealthy country, even if that child's family is poor, has a better chance of improving their situation than one born in a poorer country.

Violence is not limited to war-torn countries—certainly, children in even the wealthiest and most powerful countries in the world are exposed to violence. We just need to look at the many, many mass shootings in the United States to know this. Children in schools in the United States participate in gun drills, the way students in other countries practice learning what to do in an earthquake. In the same way, children born in these countries can also be poor or experience deprivation. But in the great birth lottery, a child who is born in a wealthy country where violence and war are far less common has won the first prize. The bonus prize is when that same child is born into a wealthy or at least more financially stable home.

Money shouldn't matter. As many have told us, we can't take it with us, so why is it important? Pretending it doesn't matter is a luxury that only those of us who have money can afford. For others, having sufficient money to be able to feed and clothe ourselves and our family is the primary reason we covet it so much. Add that to what is considered a fundamental need—that of a healthy home that only money can buy, and it's understandable that a child needs to be born, or at least raised, in a family where money isn't a constant struggle. We'll look at why it's important in the next chapter. For now, just remember that having money doesn't matter, but not having it matters a great deal.

But back to the family. We learn from our parents, and if our parents are a good influence on us, the chances are that we will learn to be good people. It's not inevitable though. Criminals are born into the most contented of households. Dennis Rader, the killer better known as BTK—Bind, Torture, Kill—had what was by all accounts a normal childhood. He was the eldest of four brothers, his parents were not known to be abusive, and they were reasonably well-off. Dylan Klebold, one of the students who committed the Columbine school shooting in Colorado in 1999, was a gifted student whose parents were actively involved in his childhood. His parents ran a real estate company, and he was encouraged to participate in sports, particularly baseball and bowling. He was said to have enjoyed them and was also involved in school productions.

Still, they are the exceptions. It's far more common to find serial killers who came from homes where abuse, both physical and mental, were inflicted on the most vulnerable. John Wayne Gacy, the "clown killer" of numerous boys and young men, was abused, both physically and emotionally, by his alcoholic father. Charles Manson, technically not a killer himself but one who persuaded his followers to kill, saw his mother go to prison when he was four and was thrown out of the family home when he was 12. Rosemary West, who, along with her husband Fred murdered eight women and children, including a couple of their own, in the United Kingdom during the 1970s and 1980s, was the child of a paranoid schizophrenic father and a clinically depressed mother.

The debate between nature versus nurture is a thorny one when it comes to crime. Most of us don't commit crimes. We can grow up in the worst of homes and still live a life that doesn't have the shadow of a jail term, or worse hanging over us. We may not even be tempted to commit a crime (not seriously anyway). It's not uncommon to have thoughts like "oh, I'd like to murder so-and-so for what they said," or "I want them to pay for what they've done." The difference is that while we have these thoughts, surprisingly few of us act on them. So why does the criminal?

A lack of empathy is often attributed to the criminal. They cannot accurately picture how their victim feels, so they don't care enough to stop and think about how the criminal act will affect others. Much debate surrounded the horrific murder of James Bulger, the two-year-old who in a notorious case in Britain in 1993, was led to his death by two boys not even in their teens. Did those boys truly understand what they were doing to the toddler? Did they understand the consequences of what they were doing as they threw rocks at a defenseless child? One of the two boys is reported to have asked an arresting officer if James had been taken to hospital to make him alive again. But at the same time, they placed James on a railway track in an effort to make his death look like an accident, so it is hard to imagine that they didn't understand that they were killing a child. The reasons behind James's murder have never been explained. Blame, of course, was thrown at the parents, particularly the parents of Robert Thompson, whose father was reported as violent and whose mother was an alcoholic. Surely, armchair critics say, the parents must have known that their ten-year-old sons had violent tendencies.

If a child has a parent who is less involved in their life or a parent who abuses them, that child may well grow into an abusive adult. It's the life they understand. They don't like it—who does?—but it's what they know and what they are used to. But to use the example of

Robert Thompson, if his parents were truly to blame for the way he acted—the almost beyond belief brutality shown toward a child by another child—surely his siblings would have done so as well? He had six of them, so the odds are reasonable that at least one of them would have also grown into a dysfunctional adult. But his brothers and sisters appear to have grown into unremarkable adults.

Or the family of Fred and Rosemary West. As mentioned earlier, Rosemary had a disastrous childhood, and Fred's wasn't much better. He claimed to have been involved in an incestuous relationship with his mother and had little education. In addition, he had a head injury in his teens, which may have left him with brain damage. So, their children lucked out when it came to parental role models. What are the odds of having not one, but two, serial killers as parents? The couple had eight children between them. Two of those children died at the hands of one or the other parent. Of the other six, most witnessed abuse or were actively abused by their parents. Fred was reported to have raped several of the daughters, and one child admitted to seeing his mother "stamp" on his sister Heather, one of the two children who were murdered. The family joke was that if they misbehaved, they would land out under the patio "like Heather." However, only one of the surviving children, a son who was convicted of sex with a 14-year-old, has been convicted of any crime as an adult.

Growing up as the child of a serial killer is, fortunately, a fairly rare event. However, children do grow up in homes where one parent subjects the other, or the children, to physical or emotional violence. While it's not inevitable that an abused child grows into an abusive adult, it's not uncommon. The child may receive less support from the parent and lacks positive role models. Neither the abusive parent nor the one who is the recipient of the abuse is seen as an ideal example for a still-developing mind. That child may resent the abused parent as much as the abusive one, especially if the abuse is shared around the family and not restricted to the adult. Why didn't the abused parent leave? Or protect the child from being abused? Yes, this is victim-blaming and shaming, but if it is what goes on within a family, it's what the child sees and interprets as normal.

The physical harm to a child growing up in an abusive household seems to go without saying. A child who is regularly being beaten will obviously suffer injuries, and the damage caused by these injuries can last long beyond the normal healing time. Brain damage is the most serious of these physical consequences, but broken bones, damage to lungs and ribs, and scarring can cause permanent harm.

The mental or psychological harm to a child is less obvious, but studies have shown[1] that the damage is just as real as the physical harm. Low self-esteem, distrust, a lack of self-control, and cognitive difficulties are recognized as some of the aftereffects of childhood abuse. So too, is the disruption to the home life when one or more parents is abusive. The family might move around, particularly if social workers or concerned neighbors start asking questions about why there are so many bruises or broken bones. Children who move around a lot lose contact with the education system, with doctors, and with other family members. They lose the wider support network that might otherwise protect them from the family abuser. When there is no coordinated system to keep track of children who are at risk, they fall between the cracks.

Substance abuse is another consequence of childhood abuse. While not all violence or abuse stems from a parent who has issues with alcohol and drugs, it is a fairly common feature. And again, the child mirrors what they see their parents do. They may also turn to drugs or alcohol[2] as a coping mechanism. Substance abuse is recognized as a leading cause of crime, as we will see in a later chapter.

Let's leave murders aside for now. The likelihood of a child growing into a criminal is raised if that child is exposed to criminals at a young age. The family is the child's first teacher, and if the family normalizes criminal activities, even non-violent crimes such as property crimes, the child will think they are okay. Or the status quo.

If a child's parent is sent to prison for a crime, they are naturally somewhat removed from that child's life. The child loses the day-to-day contact with that parent, and visiting the parent in prison if this is permitted, will not create the same bond that seeing the parent in the comfort of home can provide. Prison visits can be stressful and in some cases, the other parent is reluctant to permit these visits. The child might remain with the other parent, be placed with family members, or enter the foster system. Again, it must be stressed that none of these factors mean that the child will grow into a criminal. However, the odds increase somewhat.

The term "social learning theory" refers to how we learn behavior by watching the behavior of others. Albert Bandura[3] first proposed this theory, suggesting that in an intimate setting, like the family home, we see close-up and repetitive behavior that we then encode and, eventually, repeat. Our parents reinforce our behaviors, in theory, by rewarding our good behavior and punishing us when we demonstrate less-than-favorable traits. So if we grow up in an environment where criminal behavior is the norm or treated as a not-quite punishable offense, are we more likely to become criminals ourselves? Studies have shown[4] that this is often the case.

It seems unfair that criminal behavior is often intergenerational. Add this to the lottery effect of where we are born, and it's clear that some children really don't have much of a chance in life.

Is there anything we can do about this though? Is it enough simply to look at the adult criminal, see the childhood they had, and brush it off as inevitable? Or should we look at breaking the cycle? This is where rehabilitation can have a far more positive effect on long-term crime statistics than mere punishment. It not only has the chance of preventing the adult from committing further crimes; it can also potentially stop the children of that criminal from following in their parent's footsteps. The adult becomes a better role model for their children, who then learn more appropriate social behavior that will, we hope, prevent those children from growing into criminals themselves.

The family is so often the most important influence on a child's life. Families can make or break those who grow up within their ranks. We value the family unit, as we should. The alternatives are mass state orphanages or a "Brave New World" type of environment, where test-tube children are raised by the state, conditioned by nightly sleep learning, and taught that "mother" and "father" are swear words. Supporting the families of criminals can give society the chance to make a real difference in those children's lives, and that helps everyone.

Support comes in all forms. Creating positive role models for those children, either by rehabilitating the parent or by removing the parent (who is beyond any reasonable hope of redemption), is one. Another is by recognizing that a parent who is sent to prison will have difficulty financially supporting their family. Money, as we said earlier, talks. Let's look at the effects of financial security on crime and criminals in the next chapter.

CHAPTER 3
MONEY TALKS

"The poor you will always have with you."
~ Matthew 26:11

Ah, poverty. All criminals are poor, lower-class members of society. We live in stratified social groups where the upper class looks down on the lower class, and the lower class has no time for the poverty-stricken at the bottom of the heap. No wealthy person has ever committed a crime in the history of the world. Ever. Rich people don't commit crimes. At least not ones that they can be convicted of. Because there are two factors protecting the rich—the first being that they don't have to commit crimes in order to survive. And the second is that when they do commit crimes, they can afford the best lawyers, thus, reducing or even removing any sentencing penalty (assuming they are found guilty).

However, when it comes to who commits crimes, as opposed to who gets convicted of them, while the statistics do show that those who are less well-off commit the majority of property-related crimes, the lines start to blur when it comes to more serious crimes.

So why is a crime most often characterized as something that only poor people do?

For starters, when it comes to lower-end crimes, like those of burglary, shoplifting, and other petty thefts, most criminals are just looking to survive, and this is a struggle most often faced by the poor. If the family budget is tight, and the difference between a child being able to eat breakfast is nothing more than stealing a few items from a supermarket, the temptation is greater for the parent of that child to "remove" a few low-priced but tasty food items. Someone sure of their next meal lacks that incentive.

The difficult part, and what makes crime more cyclical, is what happens next. If the shoplifter is caught, they are likely to be prosecuted, or at any rate, charged with petty theft. They may, if lucky, get off with a warning, but it's more likely that there will be something noted against their names in official records. And it is this that can have further consequences than just stealing a few items of food or a bottle of milk.

Because we are all online these days. There are certainly people who slip under the radar or who prefer to live "off the grid" by not engaging with the likes of banks, government agencies, or Netflix. But for most of us, our information is available to anyone who asks the right questions and has the right access. This includes potential employers, landlords, lenders, and immigration officials.

We are convicted of petty larceny. We don't serve a prison term—why would anyone want us to? It was just a few cans of soup, some vegetables, and a half dozen eggs. But the conviction stands. We still need to pay the bills, and so we apply for jobs. We are granted an interview, and we get the job—hurrah! And we are asked the question: have you ever been convicted of a crime? We can either say yes, and hope that they understand or no, and, therefore, lie to our employer, hoping against hope that they don't do a background check. Of course, they might not, but if they do, there's the conviction. And we not just have a conviction for larceny; we lied about it. No job.

The same applies to when we are looking at housing. We may not be renting an apartment in the most salubrious of buildings, but even then, the landlord may ask us for references. Or when we are at the bank, applying for a loan. Will a petty conviction be enough to disqualify us either from the apartment or from getting the financial aid we need? Often, the answer is yes, or at the very least, a qualified "no." "You can have the loan/apartment, but we need more security/a bigger bond."

Suddenly that small crime committed out of desperation and need has far-reaching consequences that greatly outweigh the benefits from committing it. Those who are keen on punishing criminals for offenses will possibly say that it's a fair exchange. "Of all the preposterous assumptions of humanity, nothing exceeds the criticisms made of the habits of the poor by the well-housed, well-warmed, and well-fed." -Herman Melville.

But basically, our small crime is suddenly a major factor in our lives. We no longer have a job to go to, our housing is substandard (if we are able to get a house), and we have to struggle to make ends meet. The step on from petty larceny is the less petty sort, then the more serious crimes. And for those, we go to jail. We are away from our families, who have to find other means of support while we're in jail. When we get out, our criminal records are no longer just for insignificant crimes but for more serious ones. Even the most generous of employers are going to be reluctant to take us on. So again, we are in strife, unable to afford to stay within society's norms.

Then certain crimes are linked to lifestyles associated with poverty, and none so prevalent as that of prostitution and drug dealing. In countries where prostitution is illegal (and even where it is legal), it is not a profession that naturally attracts those who have choices. The cases of prostitutes who are able to fund a luxurious lifestyle based on being able to charge exorbitant prices for their services are rare. More often, those who become prostitutes do so because they have few other choices. The prostitute will most often offer their services while under the protection of a pimp, who takes a share of their earnings and effectively controls them. Few labor laws protect a prostitute's working conditions. If the client gets rowdy or abusive, there are no health and safety regulations. The prostitute may be able to impose some basic safety measures (such as condom use) but they have no power to enforce any such rule. (The pimp might be able to enforce these measures, particularly because they help protect their merchandise as well.) The prostitute is committing a crime just by doing the job, and so if there is danger involved with clients (prostitutes are not referred to as living a "high-risk" lifestyle out of hyperbole) they have little recourse. They can report crimes against them, such as assault and rape, but inevitably this will result in also admitting that they are committing a crime themselves. Consequently, prostitutes tend not to report these crimes. They lose their livelihood (and freedom, in some cases) if they do. They have no protection against other criminals because they themselves are criminals.

The same goes for drug dealing. We are not talking about crime syndicates where drug dealing is a major industry. More often than not, those who sell drugs do so on a small scale. If they are involved in a petty deal that goes wrong, for example, and they are robbed or assaulted, do they report that crime against them? Or is it too risky? And if the dealer is caught, they are more than likely going to go to prison, and a drug conviction is enough to prevent freedom of travel as well as being a major red flag for employers.

What are our options then? And what is it that we as members of society can do to prevent or slow this downward spiral?

Discharge without conviction for petty crimes is a start. Allowing a clean slate provision for minor crimes is another — if the criminal can demonstrate that they have lived a crime-free life for a set period, then their earlier conviction gets wiped or at least, is not disclosable. Probation rather than physical detention for crimes where the risk of harm to others is low is another possibility. So are training programs in prison for those who are convicted and serve for short periods, and a "return to work" plan for those who leave prison, so the now-released criminal has some hope when they leave. It is far better to prevent crime by helping the would-be perpetrator to find alternatives than it is to punish the criminal after the fact and after both, they and their victims have suffered.

Those who commit crimes such as prostitution and drug dealing are put into a different basket. Sending them to prison is not likely to change what led them to these crimes in the first place. Prostitution, in particular, is a crime that punishes one person but not the other—the person selling sex gets convicted, whereas the person buying sex may get off free or with a slap on the wrist. The drug dealer is selling a product that damages others, but no one is forcing those people to buy the drugs. (Drug use, in itself, is often linked to crime, as we will examine further in a later chapter). The drug dealer is little more than a conduit. For these two classes of criminals, again, a better alternative would be rehabilitation and a return-to-work program that reintegrates them into the mainstream.

Poverty is linked to crime, but it doesn't cause it, as evidenced by those crimes committed by those who appear to be financially well off. Murder, in particular, is a crime that, when a rich person commits it, is well-publicized, so it's not difficult to find examples. Back in the early 1920s, the murder of 14-year-old Bobby Franks, by his millionaire cousin Richard Loeb, and Richard's friend Nathan Leopold, was ostensibly a case of a ransom attempt gone wrong but was ultimately one committed for sheer kicks.

In a combination of celebrity and wealth, the brutal bludgeoning to death of Martha Moxley in 1975 was committed by someone who allegedly declared that he would never be convicted because he "was a Kennedy." Michael Skakel was related to the American political dynasty because his father was brother to Ethel Kennedy, widow of Robert. In addition, the Skakels were independently wealthy. However, while justice was slow, the 15-year-old girl's murder did eventually result in a conviction and lengthy sentence.

Google "Phil Spector" and two titles appear: famed music producer and convicted murderer. Spector was once best known for his work with musicians such as the Righteous Brothers, the Beach Boys, and Ike and Tina Turner, and his collaboration on several Beatles hits. However, his legacy will forever be tarnished by the murder of Lana Clarkson in 2003. He attempted to cover this up by declaring that Miss Clarkson committed suicide, but in 2007 he went on trial for her murder. The motive for her murder was not clearly established, but it has been pointed out that Spector suffered a brain injury after a car accident in 1974 and that he was also known to have threatened other women with guns.

Spector thought he could get away with saying that his victim committed suicide. Skakel thought his wealth and connections would get him off. Leopold and Loeb thought they'd committed the perfect crime. All three demonstrated what is currently referred to as the "affluenza" syndrome—where the person committing a crime feels that it's not a crime and that they are entitled to act as they do. Affluenza was a somewhat tongue-in-cheek definition used to describe those who can't understand why they are not entitled to anything they want, by virtue of their social status or because others are able to buy what they want without consequence. However, it became a less than amusing term when it started being used as a defense.

In 2013, a 16-year-old in Texas was arrested and charged with the manslaughter of four people. Ethan Couch was over three times the legal drinking limit when his car swerved off the road and hit a car that had broken down on the side of the road. The driver of that car, as well as three bystanders who had stopped to help, were all killed. This was not Couch's first driving offense, having been previously ticketed for speed and alcohol offenses. However, when he went to trial, his lawyer argued that he suffered from "affluenza" and that his parents failed to teach him responsibility. He did not accept the consequences of his earlier driving offenses, thanks to his parents' influence, and so did not understand that his drunk driving could cause serious injury, even death. Couch was sentenced to probation that included rules around access to alcohol and restricting his entitlement to drive, all conditions that he repeatedly flouted. His mother then took him to Mexico, apparently to avoid having to face the consequences of breaking probation. In other words, she further enabled his belief that he didn't have to obey the law.

A variant of the affluenza defense is when people who commit crimes receive shorter or less punitive sentences because of the negative effect of a criminal conviction on their lives. An infamous example of this was the Stanford rape case in 2015. Brock Turner was convicted of sexual assault of an unconscious female but sentenced to six months behind bars, of which he served only three. The sentencing judge stated that serving any longer than six months would have "a severe impact" on Turner's future. He was a member of the Stanford swim team, at one stage thought to have Olympic potential. His father further stated that Turner's future should not be harmed by "20 minutes of action." Ironically, this letter, along with the notoriously light sentence, probably did more damage to Turner's future than those 20 minutes. Name recognition coupled with a high placing in Google searches for sex offenders is not something that many future Olympic athletes would want.

Other accusations against the wealthy and privileged include those of rape against movie producer Harvey Weinstein and comedian Bill Cosby. Even the former president of the United States, Donald Trump, has been accused of both sex crimes and financial crimes. These high-profile cases, and many others, goes to prove that crime is not solely the prerogative of those with fewer material assets. The difference usually lies in the difficulty of conviction when it comes to wealthy criminals and the various sentences imposed in cases where convictions are upheld. The wealthy can afford top lawyers, who can dedicate hundreds of hours to their client's case. They can afford to hire experts who can testify to this defense or that obscure case ruling. They know how best to drag out a case, to raise all possible objections to prosecution, then to sentencing. And they can afford to pay large fines or settle out of court. They put so much effort into keeping their clients out of court that by the time sentencing occurs, the client might have spent so much time on probation that the judge may even allow them time off for good behavior. To paraphrase Orwell again, all criminals are equal, but some are more equal than others. In chapter nine, we're going to look at the differences in how various classes of criminals are sentenced. But for now, it's clear that while money (or lack of it) can contribute to crime, it's not the sole motivation. A far greater problem is substance abuse, and that is what we will be looking at in the next chapter.

CHAPTER 4

UPPERS AND DOWNERS

"Prohibition only drives drunkenness behind doors and into dark places, and does not cure it or even diminish it." ~ Mark Twain

How long has the human race used drugs or mind-altering substances? Literally, thousands of years. Beer, wine, and hallucinogenic plants were known as early as 7000 BCE. It's unlikely that there was any real attempt to regulate the use of either, nor were there likely to be any such institution like an addiction treatment center. We have been using and abusing addictive substances for so long that it seems bizarre that these same substances are often behind the crime. Why all of a sudden?

For starters, potency. When we first started brewing beer, we didn't make it particularly strong. Of course, we did drink more of it—back in the day, it was safer to drink beer than it was to drink water. But even then, we still couldn't get as drunk on a few bottles of beer as we can do with today's far more potent variety. It took us a while to discover the stronger, more alcoholic variants of spirits and wine. And even though the water was not particularly safe to drink at times, we were far more likely to mix our alcohol with water. We started working out how to turn plants into fermented brews, such as turning barley or rye into whisky or potatoes into vodka. We took the fruit from trees and vines and turned them into wine, cider, and brandy.

Alcohol use has always been particularly associated with religious rites and festivals. The ancient Greeks even allocated a god of alcohol and intoxication—Dionysus, also known as Bacchus. We get the term "bacchanalian" referring to a drunken, no-holds-barred party, from this god of debauchery. The Greeks were not alone, though—gods and goddesses of beer were noted in numerous African cultures. And when it came to celebrating religious rituals, one of the most common items on the agenda was a form of alcohol. Spilling alcohol on the ground was referred to as giving a libation to the gods—a gift of thanks to whichever of the gods that person worshipped. Some religions forbid alcohol on the grounds that it removes the ability of the mind to control itself, but others refer to alcohol as a gift from a deity. Jesus turned water into wine at the wedding in Cana. Wine has long formed a part of the Catholic mass and is particularly important in the traditional Jewish Seder.

Our ancestors certainly recognized the dangers of alcohol. Early philosophers such as Plato and Aristotle referred to the need to drink in moderation. And while there were noted drunkards among the early Roman emperors (the leaders, in those days, of the world), the tendency moved toward moderation and regulation. And in those days, the general population adopted the attitudes of their leaders.

So while we used and abused alcohol, and it caused its fair share of problems, it certainly was less of a catalyst for crime than it is these days.

As we grew to understand the destructive properties of alcohol, so too did we attempt to stop its use. As mentioned earlier, some religions discourage, or actively forbid, the use of alcohol, most notably for those who follow Mormonism, Methodist, Islam, and Buddhism. Doing (or not doing) something for religious reasons will work as long as that person is devout enough to embrace the rules of that particular religion.

Another common method to reduce our alcohol consumption is price manipulation. In the mid-16th century, Queen Elizabeth I used the issuing of licenses to import wine and quality spirits from the Continent into England as a great revenue source for the perennially cash-strapped crown. Adding tax to the price of alcohol is not a recent initiative.

The most notorious and one of the least successful methods of preventing alcohol consumption is to impose a law against it. Famously, the United States tried this, passing the 18th Amendment to the Constitution that did everything but forbid the consumption of alcohol. You could not sell it, import it, or produce it, but if you happened to have some, you were allowed to drink it. The failure of Prohibition to actually prevent the USA from falling into a pit of alcoholism can be demonstrated by the almost ubiquitous ability of people to get around the law. And, of course, the rise in crime. Seeing it was illegal to purchase or brew alcohol, anyone who participated in these acts was automatically a criminal. We have all seen or heard of the crime lords who built their fortunes by getting around the Prohibition laws.

Any illegal product will naturally cost more to purchase, as the vendor builds in a "danger money" element. Additionally, if it's harder to produce, it has scarcity value, which adds to the price the vendor can demand. We admire or shudder at the thought of a Van Gogh painting commanding tens of millions of dollars, but the reason these paintings go for such incredibly high prices is that there are so few Van Goghs, and there will never, ever, be any more.

What is interesting, and dangerous, about a prohibition on alcohol, or an addictive substance, is the combination of illegality and addictiveness. Addiction, as is fairly well-recognized, is something that those who suffer from it cannot control. If you are addicted to a substance or habit, you need it. You crave it, you depend on it, and you will do almost anything you can to get it. If you can get this substance legally, such as (in most societies) tobacco, it's not usually a problem. It may cost a lot of money, but you can walk into a store, hand over a wad of cash, and purchase what you need to feed or control your addiction. However, if your particular addiction relates to an illegal substance, you suddenly have a problem.

Suddenly, desperation comes into the mix. And desperation can cause us to act in ways that we would not otherwise act. Seeing we can no longer just purchase our addictive substance easily, we are forced to search for other places where we can find them. The difficulty we face adds to the price we have to pay. Because we are now desperate for substances, we not only pay extra, but we are also prepared to take risks. Quality control over what we are buying isn't something we're interested in—we just want the high.

And therein lies the rub. When we are desperate, we do desperate things. Prohibition failed, rather spectacularly, to stop people from drinking. The ideals behind Prohibition were to improve family life, end the evils of alcoholism, and reduce crime. Nice try, and we should never fault the intentions of those who proposed the bill because they really did want to improve on a social ill. But in practical terms, Prohibition failed because it tried to impose a judgment on those who weren't prepared to accept that judgment. The founders of Alcoholics Anonymous developed an approach to dealing with addiction, and one of the fundamental approaches is that the person who has a problem with addiction must want to change that problem. Forcing a change on people will simply cause resistance. "No one can tell me what I can or can't put in my body!" is a fairly common reaction, whether it's healthy foods, vaccinations, or mind-altering substances.

That is one-half of the "prohibition doesn't work" coin. The other half, and the more serious one, is that thanks to the desperation that addiction causes, there's money to be made. During war times, black markets flourish. We might think of essentials such as food or medicine as being big-ticket items on the black market, and when these essentials are scarce, they are. But also, luxury items, like perfume or sugar during World War II, are items that people will pay exorbitant sums to acquire. If we are able to supply these items, why not ask for a premium price? And seeing we can do it, why not the next person?

Suddenly, we have rivals. We thought we had cornered the market, but seeing the money is so good, others are prepared to step in. The products we are selling are still going for high prices (they are still scarce, after all) but now we have to think of ways to protect our monopoly. Like the wine importers during Elizabethan times, we don't want anyone muscling in on our territory. So we do what we can—including driving competitors off our turf, by whatever means possible. We may have glamorized the crime lords of the 1920s, the Al Capones, the mafia bosses, the Godfather, but they did use threats, violence, and murder to protect their illegal enterprises. The profits were too big to just leave to chance or to allow for genuine competition. And crime pays.

In most societies, the ban on alcohol is no more. Other addictive substances and behaviors, such as tobacco and gambling, are also legal. But even so, let's not forget that most governments use price manipulation to discourage people from indulging in these. So again, people try to work around the system to get to the addiction of their choice. When it comes to cigarettes, particularly in the USA, people will drive across state lines or sell untaxed cigarettes to get access to cheaper tobacco. Holding up small convenience stores is not a particularly lucrative occupation unless you consider that part of the haul is likely to be tobacco products. This makes it worthwhile to the small-time criminal, who can on-sell these products to the desperate smoker. Cigarettes can be sold legally, but illegal sales are lucrative enough to make the risk one that the criminal will be happy to take.

This is one side of the link between addictive substances and crime — that of the vendor. When it comes to the person who has a drug or alcohol dependency, there is another factor to consider. We spoke of how early philosophers, and some religions, condemned alcohol because of the way it affected people's behavior. Alcohol and drugs are mind-altering substances, and this is what links them to crime.

Anyone who has ever been drunk can possibly recall how the more alcohol they consumed, the fewer inhibitions they had. People say and do things under the influence of alcohol that they might otherwise not have said. The philosopher Pliny was the first to extol the "In vino veritas" motto, referring to the way that most people will tell the truth ("veritas") after consuming a few wines (the "vino" part of the motto). If we restricted our unfortunate behaviors after drinking alcohol to a few home truths, that would be one thing (although it's possible that more than a few arguments will potentially lead to violent acts). However, alcohol and drugs also remove our judgment. We react slower, we think less, we are more prone to anger, and we do things we regret. The biggest, most common problem with alcohol and crime is the fact that so many people will get behind the wheel of a car. In the USA, more than a quarter of deaths in motor vehicle accidents[1] have alcohol as a factor.

Alcohol can make us angry or irrational. Ask any person in charge of an emergency department at the hospital, and they will tell you that Friday and Saturday nights, when bars are open late, and workers head out after a week's work to party, are busy nights. We get into fights with other people at the bars, or we go home and fight with spouses (often violently) because we have consumed a fair bit of alcohol. (That's assuming we have managed to get home safely—not a guarantee given we've taken in a skinful of booze). Domestic violence soars during holidays. You would think that the likes of Christmas, the season of goodwill, would be a happy time for many. Instead, people drink more, eat more, and associate with family more. Scars that might have been covered during the year are ripped open, and, with inhibition thrown to the wind, people snap.

Then there's sexual assault. People get drunk and lose the ability to judge whether consent is actual, implied, or just not there. Other people get drunk and lose the ability to judge whether the person they are with is a safe person to be around. The would-be sexual offender might believe that they can do what they like because, hey, they're drunk, and everyone knows that what you do when you're drunk doesn't count, right? The same doesn't apply to those people who are assaulted—they should have expected this because they should have known better, and clearly, this is risky behavior. We mentioned Brock Turner in the last chapter, the young man who was convicted of assaulting a drunk (passed out) female. The female in question, like many who are assaulted in a social situation, was thought by some to bear some responsibility for what happened to her because she was clearly not making rational decisions, thanks to her alcohol-induced stupor. However, the fact that Turner had also consumed alcohol, meaning that he was not making sound judgments himself, was seen as a mitigating factor. He didn't know what he was doing, so he should not be held responsible for what he did. Sauce for the goose.

Alcohol-related crimes include armed hold-ups. It accounts for more than 40%[2] of homicides in the States. Partly this is the judgment problem—we lose our ability to think when we have consumed a few beverages, and we make irrational choices. Partly it's to do with the way that alcohol lowers our inhibitions. We lose our temper. We lash out—literally. We take offense when none is meant. If we argue with a friend or family member when we're sober, it's likely to be nasty but not lethal because the bottom line is, we love or care for that person, and we are thinking rationally. But add a few drinks into the cocktail, and suddenly, we find ourselves yelling or not being able to deal with their yelling or name-calling. So we use violence.

Even withdrawing from alcohol has its problems. Yes, we can and should encourage those around us (and ourselves) to cut back or abstain if alcohol is an issue. But we also need to recognize that the booze hasn't done our brains any favors while we've used it, and it's not going to let go without a fight. Those who quit alcohol will often suffer from delirium tremens, the "DTs," and this can cause problems such as hallucinations.

Whether we like it or not, alcohol is a legal drug in most countries. So if we depend on it, we can access it. The price may put us off, but at least we don't have to resort to bathtub gin or bootleggers anymore to get our fix. But when it comes to drugs, we are mostly looking at breaking the law. If your drug of choice is marijuana, you are reasonably lucky, as several states within the USA, such as Washington, New Jersey, and Nevada, allow marijuana for personal use. Countries like Canada, Mexico, South Africa, the Netherlands, and Spain have legalized marijuana for recreational use, and other countries, such as New Zealand, Ireland, and Israel, allow it for medical purposes. But if your preference is for harder drugs, you probably have to move to Portugal if you don't want to break the law.

The cost of drugs and the need to feed that cost is often the motive behind petty thefts. Thanks to the proliferation of consumer goods, we can't look at our television, or our computer, as a high-cost item. But stealing, and on-selling, a $500 appliance could net the drug user about $200, and that will do nicely for today's fix, thank you. The same goes for other crimes like purse snatching. How many of us carry cash these days? But if we do lose our wallets or credit cards, the petty drug user may be able to access enough cash or credit to feed a minor addiction. For a couple of days, anyway.

This book does not intend to debate the good and bad (or highs and lows, if you prefer a pun) of drugs. All we are considering here is the link between those highs and lows and the effects these have on crime. People commit crimes to obtain illegal (and therefore, expensive) drugs like heroin and cocaine. The cost of these drugs makes it alluring to people who want to make a quick buck, either selling or transporting. Perhaps if we can remove the supply and demand factor here, we would be able to break the backs of the drug cartels. Legalizing drugs of any sort would remove a large part of the profit incentive. Those who are desperate for a high would no longer have to spend exorbitant sums to feed their fix. The drug lords would lose (or at least see significant drops) in trade because if people can access drugs legally, they would not need to go to criminals.

But.

There is one drug, universally condemned, as a drug that has no merits whatsoever. A drug that doesn't just cause people to lose judgment, but to lose their minds. A drug that fries the brain. And that drug is meth**amphetamine**, also known as **meth**. Crimes committed by those under the influence of **meth** are some of the most violent and irrational crimes possible. Even meth users themselves admit that it's a violent, dangerous drug. Meth causes psychosis and a lack of rationality. The hallucinations from DTs seem mild when compared with what meth users see. While alcohol is a huge factor in murder, meth is catching up. If we are to legalize drugs, we need to be careful in deciding which ones we legalize, and few would advocate legalizing meth.

One final problem when it comes to drugs and alcohol and their connection to the crime. That is, (ironically) the lack of regulation. We expect our legal drugs, like sleeping pills or painkillers, to be prepared according to protocols and in line with safety regulations. But when it comes to illegal meds, it's a case of buyer beware. Who are we supposed to complain to if we've purchased cocaine or meth off our dealer and it turns out to be cut with baking soda or bleach? Or worse? During Prohibition, no one cared about safety standards for alcohol. How many people died of poisoning because of poorly prepared bathtub gin?

And when it comes to providing the drug, the combination of the willing supplier and the desperate buyer taps into that fundamental greed factor. If the drug we are supplying is low-risk, or even legal, such as alcohol or tobacco, we will only be able to claim a small premium for risk. But the bigger the risk, the bigger the potential profit, and the bigger effort we will make to protect that profit. That is how crime cartels are created. We love our mind-altering substances, and that love creates criminals. Either we become criminals ourselves by taking those substances, or we tap into the market to cater to our fellow humans who are addicted, or we allow those substances to take over our impulses, meaning that we commit crimes we might not otherwise have done.

So is banning drugs the best or only option? We already know that it didn't stop alcohol consumption in the States. Once we partake in illegal drugs, we technically become criminals (the clue is in the word "illegal"). And once we are hooked, we are likely to need help to get off the drugs. So we have to admit that we've broken the law in order to get the help we need. If there are good systems in place to help us get off the drugs, we can start to break the cycle. Our children won't see us off our faces, our work colleagues will trust us with important projects again, our health improves, and with all those factors in play, the likelihood of our committing any crimes while under the influence of drugs or alcohol will drop significantly.

If we are really lucky, we'll have the support to get out of the downward spiral. Or not, as the case may be. Often, it depends on the company we keep. We'll look at this next.

CHAPTER 5
IT'S WHO YOU KNOW

"If you live among wolves you have to act like a wolf."
~ Nikita Khrushchev

We have already looked at how our family influences how we turn out. Many of the decisions we make as we grow (and when we are grown) stem from the lessons we learned in the home. But other groups affect how we develop and react, and those are our peers. Our friends (and enemies), our neighbors, our romantic partners, our work colleagues, and our partners in crime will influence us, one way or the other, almost as much as our families do.

At school, it's common to join a gang. Not the kind of gang that goes out to commit crimes for kicks or to mark their turf, nor even the gang that we find in novels like "Oliver Twist" where crimes were committed primarily to survive. No, we join the gang that will give us companionship, social acceptance, protection against feeling like a loner or being a target for bullies (or, in some cases, for being the bully gang). It's a part of growing up—good or bad—and it's the price we pay to get through adolescence and make it to adulthood. Once within the gang, we take care to stay part of the group. If we get kicked out, we lose the protection that the company provides. And sometimes, the pressure of needing to stay part of the group leads us to bad decisions. "A person is smart, but people are stupid" is a fairly common axiom. We do things as part of a group that we would not do as individuals.

We want to fit in with our social peers. It's inevitable—even the most introverted of us don't necessarily like to be the "different" one as we grow up. We may be able to cope with being different when we are adults, but when we're kids? Forget it. And as impressionable kids, who want to fit in, we adopt the habits of our contemporaries, particularly if we want to stay friends with them. If one of our group (the alpha) decides that the newcomer is an oddity, they will encourage us to point and stare at that newcomer. Others follow suit. Peer pressure is real and can damage more than just that newcomer. Peer pressure leads us to enable, if not actively partake, in bullying behavior. We don't know how to stop, and we certainly don't want that bullying behavior turned in our direction. So we go along with it.

Bullying, while undoubtedly damaging, isn't generally a criminal act. Schools will try to clamp down on it because of the damage to the victim, but it's not likely to lead to prosecution. Where gang behavior, or mob mentality, becomes criminal is when the alpha of the group thinks that it would be a good idea to rob a store, or drive drunk, or pressure the social outsider in such a way that they self-harm.

Teenagers like to test the boundaries of behavior. Parents and caregivers are the most common boundary setters, but teachers and those involved in the teenager's education will at least attempt to tell their students what is acceptable and what isn't. But the teenager's brain, largely still developing, combined with pressure to conform, to be accepted, and who is stuck between not being an adult, but not quite a child either, will often find it necessary to rebel against accepted mores.

Being part of a group that commits a crime doesn't mean that everyone in the group is guilty. What it can mean, though, is guilt by association. If your two best friends spend their Friday nights on the town harassing people, breaking into stores, and being aggressive to others, and you are with them at the time, you may not be doing the criminal acts, but you are certainly not stopping it. Peer pressure means that you won't stick up for the person being harassed, the store owner being robbed, or the people on the receiving end of the aggressive behavior. You are also inviting the victims' family or friends to retaliate against you for having been a bystander, And when your friends are finally arrested for their behavior, you are probably going to be considered as "almost as bad" as your friends because (fairly or unfairly) you are seen as having enabled them.

Violence is contagious. If you see a crime being committed against a friend, you may well report it or, at the very least, intervene to try and stop that crime. But if you see a friend committing a crime, it is more common to either close your eyes to what your friend is doing or start seeing the behavior as socially acceptable. This is particularly the case in adolescents, where studies have found that younger people are more likely to commit a crime if they have witnessed a contemporary doing so[1].

Peer pressure isn't always a bad thing. Being part of a gang that values high achievement or that encourages healthy participation can improve the prospects of those gang members who might otherwise fall back. Peer pressure can stop criminal acts—if you think it's okay to drive drunk, for example, but your friends are anti, you may feel pressured into avoiding the negative behavior. Peer pressure and the desire to conform is believed to be one of the reasons that smoking, a generally accepted unhealthy and undesirable behavior, is on the wane among younger people. If you smoke, it's almost expected that you do so on your own, or at least away from others. And when you're young, do you really want to be ostracized for your habit?

The neighborhoods in which we live may influence our criminal behavior. Not necessarily because everyone in the area is law-abiding or otherwise. We have already looked at how wealth levels can influence crime levels. Just because you grow up in a less-than-salubrious neighborhood does not mean that you will automatically live a life of crime.

But where you live will often determine, not so much whether you commit a crime, but whether you are ever arrested for one. It's axiomatic in the minds of most arresting officers that if you are looking for a known criminal, the first place you check are the areas where that criminal feels most comfortable—their home, their neighborhood, and their associates. If you happen to be in the wrong place at the wrong time and bear a passing resemblance to a suspect, you may well be arrested for a crime you didn't have any involvement with, and sometimes, it's not that easy to prove your innocence. You may have a lack of understanding of your rights or may not be able to afford a lawyer who can have your case dismissed.

Assuming you are innocent, of course. It could just be your bad luck that on the day you committed a petty act of larceny, your neighbor committed a more heinous act, bringing the full force of the local police department on to bear against all known associates of that person, tenuous or not. As they swoop in on you, hoping to find something against your neighbor, they notice the proceeds from your relatively minor act. You become collateral damage from your neighbor's crime. No one is saying that you should get away with your petty larceny, just that on a different day, in a different neighborhood, that's exactly what would have happened. Guilt by association again.

But some of the most serious acts of violence are done by more than one person. One such example of this is referred to as "folie à deux" — shared madness. Folie à deux has been recognized as a psychiatric condition in which one of a pair convinces the other that their particular psychotic delusions are real. The pair can be spouses, mother and son, father and daughter, or unrelated. It is often debatable whether the less dominant person in the pair would have committed the crime had they not met or become involved with the primary partner. However, once the crime has been committed and that barrier is broken, both are usually equally enthusiastic.

Many notorious couples are examples of folie à deux, such as Bonnie Parker and Clyde Barrow, the bank robbers turned murderers from the 1930s. Barrow was a small-time criminal before he met Parker. She was living a fairly average, unremarkable life. However, as their relationship developed, so too did their criminal acts, of which they both partook. The Moors Murderers are another case in point. Ian Brady was a petty thief who spent time in juvenile detention centers before he met Myra Hindley, a typist with no criminal past. Once they became romantically involved and moved in together, however, Brady moved on from a vague idea about robbing banks to full-on criminal activity, culminating in the sexual assaults and murders of five children in Manchester, England, in the 1960s. Hindley was believed to be nothing more and Brady's enabler in the earlier crimes (he did not drive a car, so it was she who picked up their victims and brought them to him). She certainly knew the first victim, Pauline Reade, meaning that when Hindley offered Pauline a ride, she got into the car willingly. However, in the later murders, Hindley was an active participant.

It is not clear exactly why John Allen Muhammad and Lee Malvo shot and killed ten unrelated victims and injured a further three in the Washington sniper shootings of 2002. Muhammad was executed for the murders, while Malvo (a minor at the time) received life sentences. The two men were not related, but Malvo was said to see Muhammad as a surrogate father, and lawyers for the youth described Muhammad as controlling the then-17-year-old. There were suggestions that the motive for the attacks was to start a race riot and that Muhammad indoctrinated Malvo into believing a race war was necessary. Nothing in Malvo's earlier life suggested that he would turn to murder—he needed to meet his surrogate father for him to take that step.

Moving on from couples are the crimes committed by gangs. The United States Department of Justice refers to a gang as "associations of three or more individuals who adopt a group identity in order to create an atmosphere of fear or intimidation."[2] Gangs are often organized by race or ethnic groups and are identified by colors, patches, or symbols. Someone wanting to join the gang is often required to pass an initiation test, and this generally involves committing a crime. The gang's raison d'etre is often, but not always, to make money via robbery, intimidation, or violence. Some gangs include prostitution, illegal gambling, and "fight clubs" as moneymakers. They have rules that all members must adhere to or face expulsion. Gang members are predominantly male, although women may be permitted to join as associates or fringe members. And when it comes to crime, members of gangs are three times as likely to commit violent acts as non-gang members[3].

Gangs often develop as a way to protect their members, usually recruited from displaced, socially marginalized, or disadvantaged groups. Their original intentions may have been fairly noble—aimed at protecting those groups and to right the inequalities these minorities faced. But over time, their role has less been about protecting the individual and more about protecting the gang's territory. Rival gangs in urban areas fight for the control of the illegal markets, particularly the drug market. Younger people will often join gangs to gain protection and find that once in, it's hard to get out (as mentioned, initiation into a gang will often include committing a crime). A gang member may stay because their gang becomes their family and provides them with the amenities that they cannot get in "mainstream" society. They may lack work opportunities, and now that they are gang members, they probably have a criminal record, thus further reducing their chances to break away. In a 2010 report by the Federal Bureau of Investigation (FBI), crimes committed by gang members have been estimated to account for at least 48% of all crimes[4].

Gang numbers are increasing. There are approximately 33,000 gangs in the USA, with 1.4 million members. And the crimes they are responsible for or involved with are becoming increasingly sophisticated. As mentioned earlier, a lucrative market for the gangs is the drug trade, and a side market of this is money laundering. Cybercrimes are another popular method for the more tech-savvy gang member. Ransomware attacks on government departments and banks involve hackers breaking through security, accessing files and personal details, and demanding payment in return for not releasing this personal information. Organized gangs, particularly those that operate in more than one country, are usually behind people smuggling and the sale, production, and distribution of child pornography. The growth of the internet means that even with the extensive resources available to the FBI and other government agencies, the gangs are able to shut down operations in one area and start them up in another with barely a pause. Attempts to prevent or shut down these activities are often thwarted by the fact that the gangs may operate in a jurisdiction outside of government reach. The FBI are effectively playing catch-up, or whack-a-mole, with these groups, thanks largely to the money potential these illegal operations offer. If there is enough money to be made, a flexible attitude regarding the harm to victims, and a big enough pool of potential customers, gang criminals will always have sufficient motivation to want to stay one step ahead of lawmakers.

Pack crimes, as opposed to gang crimes, are where a group of people, usually friends, mob together to commit acts that the individual wouldn't normally consider. These are usually not crimes of premeditation, more of opportunity. There will often (but not always) be alcohol or drugs involved. A common example of a pack crime is when a group attacks an individual. The link between the pack can be as simple as a dislike of that individual or that the individual is available to be attacked. The pack can exhibit mob mentality: the individual loses self-awareness, so is less likely to think for themselves and lose their identity. They are more prone to emotional reactions, particularly anger or fear. When these two emotions are in control, rationality and common sense go out the window. So does any conscious understanding of what they are doing. They feel that as they are part of a group, they are bound together—everyone in the group is doing the same thing, thus, removing individual responsibility. "Seeing everyone else is doing it, why shouldn't I?" The extreme version of the pack crime is those that would also be classified as hate crimes.

Hate crimes are when the pack descends upon the individual or group who is a symbol of that which the pack hates. Crimes against ethnic minorities are often committed by the pack, as are crimes against persons because of their sexual orientation. Two particularly vicious crimes in 1998 eventually led to President Obama signing legislation specifically removing defenses against hate crimes.

The murders of Mathew Shepard, a gay man who was brutally tortured and beaten to death by two men described as homophobes, and James Byrd Jnr, a Black man who was tied to a truck and dragged to his death by three men believed to be white supremacists, were both considered to be hate crimes. The "gay panic" defense had been used to mitigate attacks against gays by those who claimed that they were afraid that their victim was making sexual advances toward them. Most hate crimes in the USA are motivated by racial bias, as in the case of Byrd, but crimes attributed to prejudice against sexual orientation are increasing. Crimes against religious groups are also on the rise; following the 9/11 attacks, those in the Muslim community were often victims of hate crimes. (We will be looking more at crimes against religious groups later in this book.) Although the Shepard and Byrd murders took place in 1998, it was not until 2009 that The Hate Crimes Prevention Act (named in honor of these two men) was signed into law.

Another common pack crime is pack rape. The common features of pack rape are a group of males, often drunk, who separate a female and attack her. They may not all be involved in the rape; it is often the case that one of the group acts as a lookout. The group will often claim mitigating factors, such as that the female was drunk or a willing participant. This particular pack crime is usually not premeditated; they tend to take advantage of a set of fortuitous circumstances, in which the female is isolated and incapable of fighting back, the males are in control, and the vicinity is secure. One or more of the males involved may claim that he was coerced into committing the rape or that he didn't see it as rape because all his friends were involved as well. Like the folie à deux couples, the individuals involved often feel less culpability because the crime was done by more than one person, and they would never have committed the crime had they been alone.

To say that we are influenced by the company we keep does not excuse our own responsibility in whether or not we commit crimes. It is a common defense to say that the criminal felt pressure to commit the act by those around them or that they were afraid. When the criminal fears retribution against themselves or a family member, they will often cite that as the reason they committed the crime in the first place. Whether this is considered to be enough of a mitigating factor is something a jury, or the judge, when it comes to what sentence to impose, will decide.

It could be that by the time we have passed our most formative years, that there really is no hope for us if we are so influenced by the company we choose to keep that we see crime as an option. We may have always had criminal tendencies, or maybe we were brainwashed, pure and simple. However, some people do retain the ability to choose, who can't claim brainwashing or the influence of others in their choices. These are the people who knowingly commit crimes because they feel they are entitled to do so as part of their job. These are the politicians, and we are going to look at these types of crimes and who commits them in the next chapter.

CHAPTER 6

IT'S ALL POLITICAL

"Well, when the president does it, that means that it is not illegal." ~ Richard Nixon

The only US president to resign from office was Richard Nixon, whose political career will always be judged by that time he turned a blind eye to actions by those in his inner circle who were so keen to see him re-elected that they decided to plant bugging devices in the headquarters of Nixon's opponents. They broke into the Democratic party headquarters at the Watergate Hotel, Washington DC, and gained access to phone lines and political documents. The depth of Nixon's complicity may not have stretched to him encouraging the break-in in the first place, but his attempts to cover it up were enough to lead to an attempted impeachment. Before he could be impeached (at the time, he would have been only the second US president to be impeached, after Andrew Johnson in 1868), he resigned from office. He defended his action to British journalist Robert Frost by saying the famous line quoted at the start of this chapter.

When political figures commit crimes, are they crimes? Are they not done for the greater good? For the good of the country or the people? Are they crimes of expedience? And can they be justified?

Political figures have committed what ordinary folk would consider criminal acts for generations. Roman emperors murdered rivals. Kings got rid of inconvenient threats to their thrones, even when those threats were members of their close family. Governments would punish parts of the country as retribution for real or perceived disobedience. Political leaders are known to have lined their pockets with public funds or used their positions to coerce money from supporters. Government agencies, acting under orders from heads of government, supported, if not actively arranged for, the murder of so-called dissidents, critics, and even the leaders of countries considered to be a threat. They also used their power to influence elections in other countries. And governments have encouraged violence against target groups, then permitted those who committed those crimes to avoid the consequences of that violence.

If you think that these are made-up examples, let's look at a few of these political "crimes' through the ages.

1) ROMAN EMPERORS AND ISSUES WITH RIVALS

Thanks to many historical dramas, including Shakespeare's play, the instance of Julius Caesar and his murder at the hands of his close friend Brutus is well known. However, it was more common for the emperor to clear away his rivals, using dubious means to have them executed. Emperors Tiberius, Caligula, and Claudius, all either actively or indirectly, had inconvenient political figures murdered. Caligula was the least subtle of the three, making no bones about murdering his sister (whom he married) and may have helped his father's murderers. He also had his co-emperor, Tiberius's son Gemellus, murdered. Tiberius gave tacit approval for the murders of his nephew (Caligula's father) and his stepsons, all more popular and seen as potential heirs (or threats) to his rule. He eventually handed over control of Rome to his chief advisor, Sejanus, who presided over the judicial murder of any who wanted to see reform in government. Claudius, who succeeded Caligula, was more tempered in his actions, but he, too, used his power to either exile, disinherit, and in the final act, execute those who could have challenged his rule. Nero ruled after Claudius, and one of his first acts was to murder Claudius's son, Britannicus, and daughter Octavia (whom Nero had married).

2) KINGS WHO HAD ISSUES WITH HEIRS

In the early 13th century, Richard II of England, better known as "Lionheart," died without issue. By the normal laws of succession, the next in line would have been his brother Geoffrey. However, as Geoffrey died before Richard, Geoffrey's son Arthur was next in line. This did not go down well with Richard and Geoffrey's youngest brother, John, who captured the 13-year-old Arthur and imprisoned him. Arthur was not seen again and was widely believed to have been put to death by his uncle. Arthur was far from the only royal with unfortunate relations—a few centuries later, King Richard III had his two nephews, Edward V and Richard of York, declared illegitimate and thrown into the Tower of London. The "Princes in the Tower" were never seen alive again—again, the general belief is that they were murdered either by Richard or on his orders. Peter the Great of Russia was the great reformer, who survived a tumultuous childhood at the hands of his half-sister Sophia, was co-heir with his sickly half-brother Ivan, and is probably best remembered for building his "Window on the West"—the city of Petersburg. However, when his son, Alexis, spoke out against his father, Peter had him tried and executed. While Henry VIII of England permitted his children to live, he was less kind toward his wives, executing two for what even at the time were considered trumped-up accusations, and when his chief advisors failed to toe the lines, he again used the court system to strip them of any wealth they had (if they were lucky) or had them executed after taking their wealth away (if they were really unlucky).

3) GOVERNMENTS THAT HAD ISSUES WITH THE CONSTITUENTS

In the mid-19th century, Ireland, then part of the United Kingdom, suffered what became known as "The Great Hunger" when the potato crop, on which most of the Irish people depended for food, was hit by a blight for four years in succession. Ireland had been somewhat forcibly included in the United Kingdom in 1801, and this was not something that had occurred peacefully or without rancor. Many leading figures in Ireland wanted to self-rule, and many leading figures in England wanted to bring Ireland into submission. When it became clear that the Irish were suffering following the first year of crop failure, the British government did take sufficient aid measures. However, as the famine dragged on, later prime ministers would withhold aid from Ireland in an attempt to force through punitive measures against landowners. So extreme were these measures that the British government would later (many years later) formally apologize for their inaction during the crisis.

In 1932, Josef Stalin, the leader of the Union of Soviet Socialist Republics, allegedly ordered that one of those republics be punished for allowing foreign infiltration in local government and claiming that the people were less than enthusiastic members of the union. The Ukraine, while briefly independent following the Russian revolution, was incorporated (forcefully) into the USSR, and this caused the leadership to doubt its loyalty. The region has long been one of the richest grain-producing regions within Russia/the USSR and has been referred to as "Moscow's bread basket." However, the feelings by the USSR's leaders that the bread basket did not support Soviet principles led to a punishment remembered as "Holodomor," the murder by starvation. While the Ukraine were still permitted to grow food, the quota that they were expected to supply and send to the rest of the USSR was set at impossibly high levels, meaning that none of the food grown could stay within the Ukraine. When aid from other countries was offered, the government refused to allow that aid into the Ukraine. Stealing food was punishable by execution, but there was often no food to steal. Horses, dogs, and humans were all consumed in an attempt to fend off the state-sanctioned starvation. There are no definitive assessments of the number of people who died during the Holodomor, but the estimates range from two to ten million.

4) POLITICIANS WITH THEIR FINGERS IN THE TILL

It is widely accepted that politicians earn a good salary but work long hours and have to deal with a level of scrutiny in their financial affairs. We vote them into office, we allow them to have power over us, and to a certain extent, we trust that they will act in the general interest of the public. But that doesn't mean that the people we vote into office deserve our trust. Power corrupts, as they say, and absolute power corrupts absolutely. Some of the more notorious recent examples of cases when the leader of the country took from the public pot include Slobodan Milosevic, President of Yugoslavia (formerly Serbia) from 1989 until 2000. Money laundering and claiming government funds for personal use by both himself and his family members would help bring the dictator down, but he is best remembered for his war crimes.

Ferdinand Marcos, President of the Philippines, took control of his country by declaring martial law, and while in absolute control, managed to embezzle billions by official means. He created corporations that claimed government funds and channeled the money for his personal use and stole money received from foreign governments, intended as aid money for the now-impoverished country. Some money was eventually returned to government coffers. However, Marcos was never prosecuted, instead dying in exile.

The prize for which politician stole the most money from his people goes to Mohamed Suharto, President of Indonesia. He claimed kickbacks from government contracts, stole money earmarked for charitable purposes, and claimed dubious tax breaks on his way to embezzling an estimated $15 billion. Some of the money has been recovered, but a drop in the ocean of what he stole. And again, he was unable to be brought to justice, as he died before he could be prosecuted.

5) POLITICIANS WHO HAD ISSUES WITH OTHER POLITICIANS, AND CRITICS

The United States has largely taken on the responsibility of "world police" since the end of the Second World War. It is the US that is largely called on by other countries to intervene when those countries have conflicts. The US tends to take the lead in wars; since the Second World War, they have been involved in wars in Korea, Vietnam, Iran, Iraq, Afghanistan, Kuwait, and El Salvador, to name a few. However, wars are generally sanctioned by the United Nations Security Council, so it can't be referred to (technically) as the US committing a crime against that country. (The unfortunate residents of the country the US decides to invade, who had little or no say as to whether the war would go ahead, would possibly disagree.) Still, there are times when the US has taken its policing role further than would normally be considered acceptable.

Much has been said about the 2016 and 2020 presidential elections in the United States. Russia has been accused of interfering with the 2016 election, and there have been many claims that the 2020 election was stolen from the then-president due to voter fraud. In neither case has any evidence been produced to verify the claims (in the 2020 case, every claim has been dismissed by the courts). However, had there been interference, it would almost be poetic justice, as the US has overtly or covertly been meddling in elections in numerous other countries. Research has shown[1] that in the years between 1948 and 2000, the US interfered in over 80 elections. Such interference includes applying pressure on international organizations to approve loans to governments run by candidates the US favors, such as happened in 1996 when President Clinton was so keen to see Boris Yeltsin, the incredibly unpopular Russian president, succeed in his re-election bid. From Clinton's point of view, Yeltsin was far more likely to work with the US than the other candidates, and that was more important to the US than whether or not Yeltsin was the right candidate for president. Clinton arranged for the International Monetary Fund to approve a $10 billion loan to Russia, thus handing Yeltsin a financial weapon he was able to use to impress the voters. The tactic worked, so much so that *Time* magazine featured Yeltsin on its cover, with the slogan "Yanks to the rescue." Helping out foreign leaders in this way may not be strictly illegal (it was hardly underhand, as the tactic was widely reported at the time) but it raises questionable moral issues.

But neither wars nor election interference is quite as illegal as those crimes when the government uses its authority to kill someone they see as a threat. In 1963, the President of South Vietnam, Ngo Dinh Diem, was assassinated, ostensibly in a coup. However, it was later discovered that the CIA, while not behind the coup, was in favor of it and gave support to those who took part. US President Kennedy was insistent that Diem be removed from power and effectively recommended the coup. That this led to Diem's death may not have been the intention, but it is hard to deny that the US played a significant part in that death.

More blatantly, the 2006 poisoning of former Russian spy Alexander Litvinenko has been squarely laid at the feet of then-Russian prime minister Vladimir Putin. Litvinenko's criticism of Putin dated back to when they were both working for the Russian Federal Security service when Putin was Litvinenko's boss. After Litvinenko left Russia in 2000 and Putin became the Russian prime minister, Litvinenko continued with his attacks on his former boss, including claims that the government was behind the assassinations of journalists who criticized the regime. When he fell ill after visiting with a former agent and a colleague, he recognized his symptoms as that of someone suffering from polonium poisoning, a substance that would not be easily obtainable without government help. His autopsy confirmed polonium as the cause of death, and investigations have concluded that Putin was behind the murder.

One final case of murder by the government was the 2018 case of Saudi journalist Jamal Khashoggi. At one time a friend of the Saudi royal family, Khashoggi grew increasingly critical of the policies of Crown Prince Mohammed bin Salman, writing regular columns for the Washington Post in which he argued against the crown prince's claims of reform in Saudi Arabia. Additionally, Khashoggi was believed to have knowledge of Saudi links to the 9/11 terrorist attacks against the US. The journalist was last seen entering the Saudi embassy in Istanbul, where he had been applying for papers to arrange for his divorce and remarriage. He was initially reported as having died during a fight, but later, Saudi officials confirmed that those within the embassy were ordered to restrain Khashoggi and bring him back to Saudi Arabia. They would claim that his death was accidental, but there was surely nothing accidental about the fate of his body, which was allegedly dismembered and disposed of at an unknown location. The crown prince has been accused of, but never charged with, arranging the journalist's death.

6) GOVERNMENTS WHO ENCOURAGED THEIR PEOPLE TO COMMIT VIOLENCE

Cases in which the government has actively encouraged their constituents, the likes of you and me, to commit violent acts against other constituents, like our neighbors, are sadly not rare. Far and away, the most well-known case of this happening was the Holocaust, which resulted in the deaths not only of six million Jews but also many members of the clergy, journalists, homosexuals, gypsies, people with disabilities, and political opponents. The first major act of violence in the Holocaust was the Kristallnacht riots, which took place in November 1938. These riots targeted Jewish-owned businesses, as well as synagogues, and resulted in over 100 deaths. However, the police and fire departments were ordered by authorities to do nothing as fires burned, and people were beaten and died. Those unfortunate victims of this violence had no recourse. Over the next seven years, the Jewish people within Germany and the countries it later invaded had no protection from the government or the authorities against further violent acts. (It should be pointed out that not all of the Axis countries followed Germany's policy—the governments and officials of countries such as Italy, Bulgaria, and Hungary did what they could to protect their Jewish citizens.) The Holocaust did not start with the gas chambers—it started with a government actively encouraging its people to either ignore what was happening to their friends, neighbors, colleagues, or family members, or in worst-case scenarios, take part in crimes against them. Within the Warsaw Ghetto, where the majority of Jews within Poland were eventually incarcerated (before being moved to the camps), this tactic extended to the creation of the Jewish Council—Judenrat—which was responsible for imposing the Nazi rules within the ghetto. Thus, the Judenrat were blamed for the conditions within the ghetto.

More recently was the "cockroaches" cry. Rwanda was a country divided by racial bias in which the majority Hutus and the minority Tutsis would often clash. The two groups are not that different in feature, but having created the divide, the prejudice remained. There had been racial tension between the two groups for decades, but this would turn into brutal tragedy in 1994. The country's president, a Hutu, and members of his cabinet died when their plane was shot down by what was believed to be a Tutsi rebel group. This turned into genocide in the weeks that followed the president's death. The rallying call came from leading government officials who wanted the Tutsi "cockroaches" eliminated, along with any moderate Hutus who got in the way. Radio programs encouraged ordinary citizens to murder their friends, neighbors, and relatives. This was done to remove the Tutsi scourge from Rwanda. The massacre was not only government-sanctioned; the perpetrators were actively encouraged to participate by being given money or food. An estimated 800,000 people were murdered in the space of a few months. This was a notorious case of both mob mentality losing its reason and government approval of mass murder.

Individuals commit crimes for reasons we have discussed or will be discussing later. They are usually penalized for doing so. However, government officials commit crimes that often go unpunished, or are even considered as justified by the standards of the time. It is also usually a government that allows a crime committed in the name of religion to be seen as less serious than other crimes. And that is what we are looking at in the next chapter.

CHAPTER 7

AS GOD IS MY WITNESS

"On the dogmas of religion as distinguished from moral principles, all mankind, from the beginning of the world to this day, have been quarreling, fighting, burning and torturing one another."
~ Thomas Jefferson

The 21st century was barely a year old when one of the most blatant acts of terrorism committed in the name of religion in history occurred. The 9/11 attacks on New York and Washington, which led to the deaths of nearly 3,000 people as well as widespread injury and damage to property, were the worst terrorist attacks in US history and the most deadly daily death toll of any act since World War II when Pearl Harbor was bombed. In the words of their leader, Osama Bin Laden, the attacks, carried out by Bin Laden's religious fanatic group Al-Qaeda, were in retaliation for the "Zionist crusader alliance and their collaborators."

But there were many acts of violence committed in the name of religion before 9/11, and there is no indication that these will stop. There seems to be a belief held by those who commit these crimes that it's not a crime if it is done in the name of a deity. (Perhaps they should go into politics.) Even in Biblical times, it was considered okay to commit crimes as long as it was done to adhere to religious laws. In Exodus, in the Old Testament, God is said to have ordered the death of first-born sons to punish their parents during the plagues. This punishment was targeted to force the Egyptian Pharoah's hand into releasing the Jews from slavery. Noble intentions, maybe, but murdering children to further a religious cause, one would have thought, should have been a no-no.

Moving past Biblical times, we continue to find examples of cases where crimes were committed in the name of a deity, and therefore, considered justified by their perpetrators.

It has a grand-sounding name, but the Crusades, which began at the end of the 11th century, was anything but a heroic mission. The Crusades began when the pope of the day urged Christians to rise up and support their fellow Christians in a war against the Turks (Muslims) over control of the "Holy Land" (Jerusalem and its surrounding area). One by-product of the fight against the Muslims was that it offered a handy excuse to also kill some Jews, with Crusaders conducting massacres as they progressed toward Jerusalem. On arrival, after the city fell, the Crusaders slaughtered the Jewish and Muslim inhabitants, estimated at 40,000. They went on to create and rule over the Crusader states in the Middle East. Various popes over the next two centuries would continue to call for Crusades, and the Christians would continue to heed the popes' call. The Crusades would not end until the fall of the Crusader states in 1291.

The Catholic church in the Middle Ages considered heresy to be a threat to society and to the church's control over that society. Therefore, it must be rooted out, and what better way to do so than to arrange for those who they suspected of heresy to face an inquisition into their beliefs? Consequently, the pope of the day authorized the creation of a "holy office of the Inquisition" to locate those who dared to think differently about church policies and beliefs. If the heretic was convinced of the rightness of the church by the end of their "inquisition," the job was done. If, however, the heretic continued to hold beliefs that were contrary or different to those held by the church, sterner measures were required. Heretics were sometimes sent into exile, presumably to a country that fitted their belief system better or one in which the Catholic church had no power. However, the more common punishment for heresy was to be burned at the stake. The assumption here is that burning at the stake was chosen partly to submit the heretic to a horrible form of death that would mimic what that heretic would be experiencing for all eternity. It was also designed to serve as a deterrent, reminding those who watched the heretic burn of what was in store for anyone who dared to believe differently than the accepted norm. Death tolls vary, with the most infamous inquisition, the Spanish Inquisition, accounting for anywhere between 30,000 and 300,000. It continued for over 300 years and not formally being abolished until the 19th century.

In the Salem witch trials in Massachusetts in the late 17th century, 14 women and five men were put to death for the crime of witchcraft. In a community where Puritanism was the main religion, anyone who didn't fit in with the prevailing beliefs was regarded with great suspicion. In none of the cases was evidence produced that we would expect in a court of law today. There was no physical evidence, confessions were coerced under torture, and statements from children as young as four were accepted. "Spectral evidence"—evidence that was based on dreams and visions—was admitted into court, much to the horror of the then-president of Harvard, who said, "It were better that ten suspected witches should escape than one innocent person be condemned."[1] The community of Salem may have believed it was acting to prevent the Devil from gaining traction in its community, again, not a bad thing, but the methods they chose to protect their community in the name of God were, and remain, a crime against those who were accused, and in some cases, executed. The death toll from Salem's witch trials is substantially below those of other trials throughout Europe, and it should come as no surprise that the people most commonly condemned as witches were women, long blamed for humankind's exile from Eden.

Jihad has become a well-known term, usually used to imply violence, but once upon a time, it simply meant "struggle." For some, protecting Islam against the infidels is considered so important that its adherents will conduct suicide missions. We opened this chapter with the most famous suicide mission of all, that of the 9/11 terrorist attacks against the United States, resulting in the deaths of over 3,000 people. Much has been said and written about that attack, but understanding why people consider that those of other faiths should be murdered is still a mystery. But the 9/11 attacks were a foretaste of other jihadi acts committed to, presumably, make Islam look more appealing. Or, at the very least, frighten people into joining. It should be emphasized here that these acts, while committed in the name of religion, are not condoned by the religion itself. Here are just a few.

In 2002, a popular holiday resort in Bali was bombed, killing over 200 people. The idea was, purportedly to defend the people of Afghanistan against America; however, the majority of those killed were Australian. In 2004, ten bombs went off in the train station in Madrid, Spain, causing the deaths of 191 people. The following year, it was London, England's turn to have its transport system bombed, resulting in over 50 deaths. All were attributed to the Al-Qaeda group that claimed responsibility for the 9/11 attacks.

In 2008, in Mumbai, India, Muslim extremists killed over 170 people in coordinated attacks. A different group claimed responsibility for this attack, but the principle remained the same—killing in the name of religion. And again in France, in 2015, 130 people at concerts, a soccer match, and bars in Paris were murdered in the name of jihad.

Gruesome murders of hostages also proved a popular way to get the message across that all bar a few had the right idea as to what religion should rule. Following the US invasion of Iraq in 2003, Jordanian Abu Musab al-Zarqawi created the religious zealot organization that we now refer to as ISIS or Daesh. al-Zarqawi's terror group was responsible for the murders of Iraqi and US civilians and officials. They have been accused of genocide against the Yazidi, a minority religious group based in Northern Iraq. They claimed responsibility for a suicide bomb attack on three hotels in Amman, Jordan, in 2005 that resulted in 60 deaths, plus numerous other attempted bombings in that country. Jordan was allegedly selected for these attacks as al-

Zarqawi disapproved of the country's peace treaty with Israel. Shia pilgrims in the holy city of Karbala, Iraq, were killed in bomb blasts in 2004, in what was thought to be for no other reason than to create strife between the Shia and Sunni religious groups. But the most common technique used in an attempt to terrorize was the graphic videos of hostages' deaths. Muath Kasasbeh, a Jordanian pilot, was burned alive in a cage, a death recorded on video by his captors and later released. Nicholas Berg, an American civilian, was beheaded, again on video. British aid worker Alan Hemming was also beheaded on camera. A common theme in these and many other videos was to parade the hostage in front of the camera, have them make a statement denouncing the West and infidels, blame leaders of countries such as the USA or the United Kingdom for their fate, and then having made their statement, to be murdered. Although al-Zarqawi was killed in 2006, the group he founded continued to operate until 2019, when US, Iraqi, and Syrian forces declared the group to have been defeated.

The Boko Haram group aims to create an Islamic state in Nigeria, with a twist—it is to be under Shariah law, the ultra-strict regime that bases its laws on the Qu'ran. One of these laws is that women captured in battle are considered sex slaves. With this in mind, Boko Haram (a name that translates to "Western education is sin") committed its most notorious crime to date—the kidnapping of over 270 schoolgirls in 2014. Based on the accounts of those who have escaped or been rescued, the girls were systematically raped, and many became pregnant. While many of the girls have been returned to their families, at the time of writing, the fate of over 100 of these girls remains unknown.

Cartoonists have taken on the challenge of making their targets equal-opportunity objects of fun. They mock presidents, sportspeople, royalty, and religious leaders. However, it was considered a bridge too far when they started mocking the founder of Islam, Muhammad. In 2005, the Danish newspaper Jyllands-Posten published cartoons making fun of the prophet. Even drawing him is considered blasphemy (although it has to be said, seeing no pictures of the prophet exists, how would anyone know what he looked like? That could have been anyone's face in those cartoons!) The cartoonist received death threats and lived the rest of his life under police protection, and riots sparked in anger from the publication resulted in over 100 deaths. One of the newspapers that reproduced the cartoons was Charlie Hebdo magazine, headquartered in Paris, France. In 2015, following further cartoons by the magazines that were considered offensive to the terrorists, the magazine's headquarters were attacked. Several cartoonists, the editor, as well as police and civilians who were caught up in a supermarket hostage situation that has been linked to the Charlie Hebdo attacks were killed. These people died because someone got offended by a cartoon that wasn't even remotely religious.

We mentioned the Holocaust in the last chapter, a genocide that occurred largely against one religious group and race. However, the Holocaust did not occur in a vacuum. The hatred of Jews is almost as old as Christianity. They were blamed for crucifying Christ, but that was just the start. There is a reason that antisemitism is regarded as the oldest hatred. The Jews were the traditional target of higher taxation in the Middle Ages because of their presumed wealth and punishment for being moneylenders (an occupation forbidden to Christians). They were kicked out of England, were ordered to convert to Christianity in other countries, and were traditionally the group to blame when anything horrendous occurred. No accusation, no matter how ludicrous, was too outrageous to fling. Jews sacrificed babies and baked the dead babies into bread. They used the blood of Christian children in their rituals. They were servants of the Devil. They brought the Black Death, the plague that killed a third of the population of Europe in the 14th century. It is hardly surprising that when the Jews were targeted for acts of violence, they were considered fair game. The late 19th century saw the rise of pogroms, a Russian term meaning "to destroy, to wreak havoc, to demolish violently." Kristallnacht, mentioned earlier, was one such pogrom, but they frequently occurred in Russia, the Ukraine, Belarus, and Poland.

Terrorism is not the only time when people feel the need to take their religious beliefs and use them to justify crimes. Churches set moral standards by which they expect their adherents to follow, and any deviation from those standards can have tragic consequences. The fear of many women who became pregnant out of wedlock would drive those women to take extreme steps to avoid the stigma, thus, the rise of backstreet abortionists. Women preferred to risk the danger to their lives by submitting to unhygienic and illegal methods of abortion, rather than facing the ostracism their church (Catholic and Protestant) would submit them to. In extreme cases, the woman would commit suicide, an act that not only took her life but also, in the eyes of the church, her immortal soul. She would be denied Christian burial.

Abuse of children by priests and members of the clergy is bad enough, but the fact that the church will often cover up the abuse to protect those clergy is almost worse. The common reaction when a religious figure was accused of abuse was initially to ignore it. In the 1950s, the Catholic church started trying to rehabilitate the priest at fault while still ignoring the damage done to the child involved. The priests were referred to treatment centers where code words such as "tickling" and "wrestling" were used to hide the reality of the abuse. However, there is no indication that the priests were ever successfully rehabilitated, leading to the next stage—the coverup, usually in the form of hush money. So widespread was the hush money tactic that the Vatican ordered their lawyers to check their insurance policies to minimize liabilities.

But abuse of this scale would not be covered up forever, and by 1992 the victims were refusing to be silenced. The courage of these victims led to others speaking up until even the power of the Vatican was unable to suppress their voices. And finally, this brought about change. A priest who was accused of abuse was not automatically relocated to another diocese, where his history was unknown. The church has been held financially accountable for the coverups and the then-pope, John Paul II, made a formal apology to all victims in 2008.

People who are sinners in the eyes of individuals or who dare to move outside what their religion deems acceptable are considered fair game to the extremists. The Taliban, an ultra-strict religious entity that took over Afghanistan in 1996, introduced Sharia law to the country. Under Sharia law, females over the age of ten were not allowed access to education. While the Taliban was overthrown following the US invasion in 2001, it remained a presence in the Middle East, particularly in Pakistan. Therefore, when a young Pakistani girl spoke up about the rights of girls to be educated past the age of ten, it made her a target. Malala Yousafzki was shot and left for dead by a Taliban extremist in 2012. While she survived, other school children targeted by her would-be assassin were less fortunate. In 2014, 150 students and teachers were killed in Peshawar, Pakistan, in an attack masterminded by Taliban extremists.

Abortion is an emotive topic at any time, bound to raise the ire of the pro-and anti-choice groups. However, nothing excuses the violence against abortion clinics and those doctors who perform abortions. These crimes include the harassment of anyone entering the clinics, arson attacks on the clinics themselves, vandalism, death threats, and in some cases, bombing. Medical staff involved in these clinics have been injured or killed. Eric Robert Rudolph, the man behind the Atlanta Olympic bombing in 1996, also targeted women's health care clinics in Atlanta, Georgia, and Birmingham, Alabama. (He also claimed responsibility for bombing a lesbian bar in Atlanta.) These were done in the name of the "Army of God."

Certain religious groups are more vocal than others when it comes to hate crimes against specific members of society. The Westboro Baptist Church (WBC) is famous for its website "God hates fags" and picketing the funerals of soldiers killed in Iraq. They blame the likes of the 9/11 terrorist attacks on the United States' support of homosexuality. The WBC has not committed any crime outside of harassment, but they have made it clear that the reason they are harassing individuals, businesses, and funerals is for religious reasons. Their founder, Fred Phelps, is quoted as saying, "God is visiting the sins upon America by killing their kids with IEDs, and the more, the merrier." And in case the Jews were worried that WBC was ignoring them, Phelps issued a press release that included the statement, "God hates these dark-hearted rebellious, disobedient Jews."

Religion, or specifically, hatred of a particular religious group, has been behind murders committed by individuals, as opposed to groups. In the United States, post 9/11, the attacks and murders on Muslims and some who looked Muslim rose from being one of the lowest noted to be the second-highest (just behind attacks on Jews). Balbir Singh Sodhi, who was actually Sikh, was murdered on September 15, 2001, in retaliation for the 9/11 attacks, and there were over 400 hate crimes reported in 2001 alone.

Mass shootings are not that rare in the United States, but church shootings are relatively so. Sometimes the shooter's motive is racial, as Dylann Roof's was when he killed nine people at a church service in Charleston. Most of the attendees were Black, and Roof is a known white supremacist. But at the Tree of Life Synagogue in Pittsburgh, 11 people were shot and killed by Robert Bowers, who yelled, "All Jews must die" as he fired. It could be argued that Judaism is a race as well as a religion, so whether these people died because of their ancestry or their religious practices is debatable. However, one particular mass shooting due to a person's hatred of another religion didn't occur in the United States, but instead, in Christchurch, New Zealand. There, in March 2019, 50 members of two mosques were shot and killed in the name of Islamophobia.

Is there any cure for these crimes committed in the name of religion? Unlikely. Exposure to different cultures and groups may help to widen the experiences, and therefore, possibly the tolerance, of those who are leaning toward prejudice, but those who are already fanatical in their belief are often so mired in the belief of their own righteousness that they are unreachable. The challenge is in how to prevent those extremist views from spreading. Too often, those who buy into the most violent of beliefs do so because those beliefs answer their social or emotional needs. Or it could just be that these people have nothing better to do with their time and fell into extremism out of boredom. Keeping busy is more than just having enough work to do—it's one way to avoid getting into crime, as seen in the next chapter.

CHAPTER 8

TIME ISN'T ON MY SIDE

"Idle hands are the devil's workshop."
~ Chaucer

We tend to think of criminals as largely coming from the ranks of the unemployed. Who else has time to commit crimes? We have already talked about how poverty plays a role in whether or not we commit crimes. Poverty is a serious driver of crime because it drives us to desperate acts, sometimes simply in order to survive. But boredom and lack of motivation, or despair, can also cause us to act in ways we wouldn't normally.

When we are employed, our boss will normally have inserted some clause like a "good behavior" bond in our contract. Before we got the job in the first place, they probably did a background check on us and found that we were clean(ish), so on that basis, we were hired. And once hired, we became a representative of our employer's brand. We might have been allocated a uniform with our employer's logo. If we have an email address, it will almost certainly include a @companyname as part of that address. If we post on social media that we are an employee of this company, we link ourselves to them publicly. So the last thing our boss will want is for us to commit a crime and have our name reported in the media as "employee of @companyname." We are obliged as part of our contract with our employer to stay out of trouble, for their benefit as much as ours. Committing a crime (depending on the nature) is likely a sackable offense. So we have an additional incentive not to commit one—our job will be on the line if we do. But take that job away, and where is that incentive?

Additionally, when we work full-time, we probably don't have the *time* to commit any serious crime. Not one that involves any level of planning, anyway. We spend most of our day at work; we commute to and from, and by the time we get home in the evening, who has the energy? Workers can and do commit crimes, of course. They come home from work tired, frustrated from their day—perhaps they had a run-in with the boss or a co-worker or made a serious mistake that earned them a reprimand. At home, they take that frustration out on the family. Or they let their hair down after a week at work, knock back a few drinks at the bar, and get into a fight. Working does not prevent us from committing a crime. It merely lessens the window of opportunity in which we have the chance to do so.

But what happens when we are unemployed? If we are lucky, it's a short-term situation. We lose our job for whatever reason (recession, a change of focus, the field we are in is no longer relevant, a pandemic, or something we've done), but we find a new one almost before the pay from the last job runs out. But more often than not, unemployment lasts for long enough for some financial bite to kick in, and once we are in a situation where we are struggling to pay for essentials, we are potential criminals out of sheer desperation. In Chapter three, we talked about this when we mentioned the common link between poverty and crime (particularly property-related crime — petty theft, shoplifting, and burglary). So we're not going to go back over the whys and wherefores of this here.

But what else are we when we are unemployed? If we go from having a full-time job that occupied a good part of our week to having little or nothing to do, we might enjoy the break for a bit. It might be a good time to get those jobs done around the house that we had been planning to do. Or we could finally have the time to work toward our goal of getting fit. But after a while, we realize that no, downtime isn't what it's cracked up to be by those who are in paid employment. It can be flat-out boring. And frustrating.

Just having to apply for jobs can be time-consuming. We have our curriculum vitae and our cover letters prepared, but we have to tweak them slightly every time we apply for a job because what is important to *this* particular employer will be irrelevant to *that* one. In a competitive job market, tailoring our CV to the job we are applying for is crucial. Employers get so many applications that they tend to only focus on the ones they can quickly assess as having visible potential.

In our first flurry of post-job optimism, we probably did do all the things we thought we'd do if we had a bit of downtime, plus we applied for a range of jobs every day. But after a few weeks, our optimism is somewhat soured as we have had setback after setback.

We start to lose confidence. We also have run out, or are close to running out, of money. So we get scared—what if I NEVER get another job? What then? How will I cope? What about my family? They depend on me, and I have let them down.

Then there's the frustration. Hey, look at my colleague who lost his job at the same time as I lost mine. How come he got re-employed so fast? What has he got that I haven't? Why did I miss out on this job—it was PERFECT for me. I could do it in my sleep! Why can't I even get an interview or a callback for any of the 15 jobs I applied for this week? Could someone, anyone, just acknowledge that I have applied for a job at your company? A little courtesy wouldn't go amiss. Why should I bother?

The incentive to get out of bed in the morning starts to wear off. As we get more frustrated and depressed, we might find that we are drinking or taking drugs, neither of which actually improves our depression or frustration levels. They can also add to our anger levels, and neither is any good for our wallet. We might start to feel that we are no longer worthwhile members of society. In a world in which status is almost always linked to wealth, we have little value. Our opinion of ourselves and how we live is almost inextricably entwined with how we provide for ourselves and our families. At the risk of including an outdated sexist view, this is especially important if we are male. Traditionally, males are the ones who protect their families, and protection includes putting food on the table. If we are male and we lose our protective role, who do we become? And as we mentioned in the first chapter, males are far more likely to commit crimes.

Being cut off from a regular source of employment can also mean being cut off from company. We do not all crave company—some of us are perfectly happy on our own. But even then, we might enjoy the odd get-together or catch-up over coffee. If we had few friends or acquaintances outside of work, then losing our job might also mean losing that social contact.

We look around the area in which we live and realize that are no jobs going, but in the area a few hours away, there might be a better chance. So we pack up and move to that area. As anyone who has ever moved house or town is fully aware, just the fact of moving is costly. If we rent, we are likely to need a bond. If we own our home, we have to sell in our area (which, seeing it's a high-unemployment area, will probably mean selling at a loss) and buy in the new area (at a higher price than what we get for our old place). We have to physically move our possessions, and seeing we can't afford movers, we have to do this ourselves. We also have to move mentally—we have to find places in our new area where we can send the kids to school, shop for groceries, attend religious services, or any number of things we have gotten used to in our old area. We lose contact with our friends and neighbors as well—our social connections that helped us through our first period of unemployment.

But now we are broke, have lost confidence, and are getting bored and frustrated. Our self-image is shattered. We are lonely, possibly drinking at an unhealthy rate or taking too many drugs. And we are afraid. This is not a good mix. Our anger levels rise the more frustrated we are, and when we are angry, our emotions take over. We think less rationally, and when we add fear into the mix, it's a cocktail of negative emotions. If all we do while in this state is to kick the chair in frustration at yet another "no" from a job application, we are probably doing quite well (although our toes might hurt a bit).

As an unemployed person, we have no legal access to a living wage. We might be able to draw on unemployment insurance or benefits, but even then, is that sufficient or sustainable? Would it be so surprising that we feel the urge to access a living wage illegally? It's not as though our boss can sack us if they found out! And hey, some criminal activities take time to arrange, and, well, we've got time on our hands.

So we start using our undeniable skills on the computer to create hacking opportunities. We find a use for that patch of garden and start growing weed for sale. We start checking out security at a local firm where we know there are cash or cash-equivalent stocks just there for the taking. We run illegal games and collect money from gamblers. We create and sell false identity documents or figure out ways to rip off the system.

So far, we have only really looked at those who went from having a steady, reliable source of income to those who have none. This ignores the connection between youth offending and unemployment. Crime is essentially a young person's game, particularly a young man's game, as we discussed in Chapter one. When we are young, we don't have the same control over our impulses that we develop as we age. We are likely to act impetuously, without any level of thinking or engagement in what we are doing. We also lack the "disincentive" or reason not to commit a crime that an older person might have—

namely, the need to support a family and maintain a clean criminal record for the benefit of future employers. We are more affected by what our peers are up to, and so if we get into a gang or "fall in with a bad crowd" as our mothers might have warned us against, we are more likely to do what we see our friends and associates do. And if we are a group of unemployed young males, frustrated and angry, we are almost a cliché when it comes to crime stats.

The types of crimes we might commit can be loosely categorized as crimes of motivation and crimes of opportunity. We are motivated to commit a crime by circumstances—we choose to drink and drive, we lift the gun and fire, we decide to rob a convenience store, we see a vulnerable person and abuse or hit them. And when we are unemployed, our circumstances include fear of financial insecurity; thus, our motivation to commit the likes of property crime so we can meet basic needs increases. Given we have time on our hands, we now also have the opportunity to commit these types of crimes.

Unemployment is usually an indicator of how the economy is doing—when the economy is strong or the country is going through a boom period, our chances of finding work are far higher. We are also less likely to see inequality when the economy is doing well. If the rich are the only ones getting richer, it's usually because the economy is doing poorly. Inequality can lead to resentment and envy, a case of "why can't I have those things?" And when we resent those in our communities who are able to easily afford to replace consumer goods, it is also easy to get in the mindset of "well, they have insurance, they won't miss a few of their possessions. In contrast, I can't afford to get my kids these things. So why not redistribute the wealth somewhat?"

The other part worth mentioning about the link between crime and unemployment is that we are affected by where we live. If we are unemployed, we are hardly likely to be able to afford to live in the more up-market areas, so our neighbors and associates are likely to be financially less well-off. It may be an urban myth to say that drug dealers can be found on the street corner of any poor neighborhood, but it's been demonstrated that it is far easier to find a drug dealer in a less salubrious area than in a wealthy one. Rich people take drugs, of course, but they tend to have the wherewithal to access the more upmarket dealers.

People in poorer areas might have the incentive, but not the ability, to adequately secure their possessions. A wealthy person can afford not just a good set of locks but also burglar alarms and security systems. Not to mention that the police do tend to take more notice of strange activity in a wealthy area, so anyone lingering with nefarious intent is likely to be noticed. In less well-off neighborhoods, it's not unusual to see groups out on the street during the day (remember, they are unemployed), and the police wouldn't think twice about any such gathering. If you walk along that street and encounter that gang, you might get wolf-whistled or heckled in some way. But you might also be robbed or assaulted, and the police are probably nowhere in sight. Your home is vulnerable to burglars because you can't afford to replace that broken windowpane or get a decent lock on the door. Businesses in the area might have inadequate surveillance systems, so they are an easy target for thieves or armed robbers. So when you live in a poorer area, you are not only more exposed to people who commit crimes, but you are also likely to be the victim of one.

And if you, or your teenage or almost adult male child, are surrounded by those who are able to make a living out of crime, is it too hard to imagine that you or your son will be tempted to join their ranks? Especially if you have been the victim of a crime. You join because when in Rome, you do as the Romans do. Or because it's safer to be on the giving end than on the receiving end.

There have been numerous studies investigating the link between unemployment and crime levels—enough studies to demonstrate that there is a clear link between the two when it comes to property crimes. The link is less clear when it comes to more serious crimes, such as violence or fraud. We might have the motivation to commit violent crimes when we are unemployed, especially seeing we have those churning, negative emotions going on, but our likelihood of doing so is far more dependent on our personality and impulse controls than on our employment status.

There is also an element of "chicken and egg" to the link between unemployment and crime. Are we unemployed because we committed a crime, or did we commit a crime solely because we are unemployed? If the latter, then it's more likely that we would have committed the crime anyway—if the only thing that stopped us from stealing, or assaulting, or raping, was that we were employed, then we only ever had a tenuous hold on our criminal behavior. Of course, if we robbed our employer, or breached their code of conduct by committing a crime while in their employment and lost our job as a result, then we certainly can't blame unemployment for leading us toward crime! But if we commit crime because we are unemployed AND we have other reasons, such as stress, fear, or desperation, as our motivations, then maybe it was the unemployment that tipped us over.

One last point about unemployment and crime and that is about the connection between high levels of unemployment and the likelihood of individuals committing crimes. When our economy is stagnant, or we are in a recession, we can become frustrated and angry. We see our government as being unwilling to help us, so why should we help them? We disconnect from society because what has it done for us? We blame others, especially the government, for not doing more to help those of us who are struggling at the bottom of the heap. And we become resentful, sometimes dangerously so. If only a few of us are in our position, then it is easier to think that "maybe it's me, maybe I can do something about my situation." Whereas when a lot of us are unemployed, we start fighting over a few scraps of jobs, we fight among ourselves, we turn on each other, and we resent those who are not in our situation. We lose the ability to empathize with others because, in our desperation, it is everyone for themselves. And we take that desperation out on others.

So what can we do about it? Not a lot, in all likelihood. For starters, unemployment will never go away. Even in the most booming of boom times, some people cannot find work or are unsuited to work. That doesn't make them criminals—it just means that they are unemployable. Then there are people who have seasonal employment only, and the rest of the year, they struggle. Are they likely to turn criminal in the off-season? Again, probably not, depending on their personality and natural tendency toward committing crimes. But when times are good, we can try and take the opportunity to safeguard ourselves against the possibility of losing our jobs. If we can afford to, that is. Insurance, savings plans, and retraining opportunities are options that might be out of our reach even when we are working full-time. More often than not, we are lurching from payday to payday and don't have the luxury of planning. And the government can't be expected to do everything.

But there is one area in which the government can improve the chances of us becoming criminals, and that is to take a good hard look at who is being incarcerated and why. That's the focus of our next chapter.

CHAPTER 9

LIBERTY AND JUSTICE FOR ALL

"All men are created equal."
~ Declaration of Independence

It is a truth universally acknowledged that while the Declaration of Independence, the United States' Founding Document, might have been all about equality, the US did not really practice what it preached. At the time of its writing, in 1776, there were over 60,000 slaves in the US, most of whom originated from African countries. The person who wrote that all men are created equal—Thomas Jefferson—owned slaves himself, as did the majority of those who signed his Declaration of Independence. There is also the self-evident statement that all *men* are created equal, no mention of women's rights here.

Atticus Finch, the lawyer in *To Kill a Mockingbird*, argued against the premise that all men are created equal. His justification for this was to point out that there are opportunities open to some but not others, intelligence levels vary, some men earn more, and some women bake better than others. Leaving aside the slightly sexist connotations here, he had a point. We are not all Olympic athletes or premier sportspeople. There are only a few of us who are talented in the acting, singing or writing departments. There was only ever one Van Gogh. But Atticus's point was that whether or not people are created equal, they had the right to be treated as equals. And this doesn't happen a lot, especially when it comes to race.

The USA, like Canada, Australia, New Zealand, and other countries originally popular with emigrants from the United Kingdom, has long struggled with how to deal with the original inhabitants of the country invaded colonized by the UK. Native Americans, First People (Canada), Aborigines (Australia), and Maori (New Zealand) have more in common with each other than just being displaced by the British conquests of the 18th to 20th centuries. They are also all over-represented in every negative statistic when it comes to measuring welfare. Each group has a lower life expectancy, an average lower-income, and education level, and score poorly in health measures. And in Canada, Australia, and New Zealand, the majority of those in prisons come from one of these groups. The exception is in the USA when it is the descendants of the former slaves who outrank Native Americans (just) in the prison population.

One other thing these groups have in common is their skin color. The darker the hue, the longer the queue to the prison door. Do people of color (PoC) really commit more crimes than other racial groups? Or are they an easy target because of their color?

We already mentioned that the indigenous people of a country frequently fare worse in health and wellbeing measurements. We also, in earlier chapters, examined the links between poverty, displacement, family dynamics, and crime statistics. So it should come as no surprise when the statistics also demonstrate that PoC are incarcerated at higher rates on average than other groups. They tend to be less financially stable, with the associated pressure that a lack of money brings. The average PoC will have a lower education level than other groups, and this limits the job opportunities. An unstable home life due to pressures of having to "follow the money" can lead to PoCs disassociating from their support groups.

And let's not forget that while colonization, particularly in the USA, is celebrated, it wasn't that great an experience for those who were there first. Native Americans were forced off their lands into tribal areas. The colonists brought diseases—some estimates have the Native American population reducing by as much as 90% when they were exposed to smallpox and other diseases to which they had no natural immunity. The colonists imposed their own brands of religion, making a mockery of the indigenous people's belief systems. The introduction of alcohol did little to improve the native people's health or wellbeing.

The imported slaves also had a rough time of it. Even leaving aside the fact that until the second part of the 19th century, another person could legally own them, the US experience for the Black person has never been one of wine and roses. Post-Civil War, the Ku Klux Klan tapped into a fear and resentment of the former slaves. Margaret Mitchell tried to glamorize the Klan in *Gone with the Wind*, describing the group's members as being patriotically and chivalrously driven into protecting their women against the raping and beating of these Civil War widows and orphans were subjected to at the hands of the freed slaves. However, the lynching of approximately 2000 Black men during the Reconstruction period was disproportionate, to say the least. And when the Klan reformed in the 1920s, the lynching continued.

When it comes to voting, the USA adopted a staggered approach to universal suffrage. In the early days, only land-owning or tax-paying white males could vote. In some states, Black men or widowed women could vote, but this would not last. It wasn't until 1870 that Black men were technically granted the right to vote (a few short years after it became illegal to own them), and even then, various states would do what they could to disenfranchise this group. The voting laws were amended to only permit citizens to vote, excluding the likes of Native Americans and other minority groups like the Chinese. From 1870—1920, states would grant, then remove, women's right to vote. Even after the universal franchise was granted, individual states used other methods, like literary tests and poll taxes, to make it harder for women or minorities to vote. It was not until the Voting Rights Act of 1965 that all the hindering methods were finally thrown out, protecting the voting rights for all groups.

One side effect of not being able to register to vote is the inability to serve on juries. When a crime was committed, and the case went to the jury, odds are the defendant would be judged by a jury of white males.

Segregation— the belief in "separate but equal" was another tool used, predominantly in the South, but extending to federal workplaces following the election of Woodrow Wilson as president in 1912. Not being able to vote also made it difficult to serve as a legislator, so the chances of being able to influence political change were reduced.

The "Great Migration" started in about 1914, and initially, more than one million Blacks left the Southern states to move into cities in the north, predominantly New York, Detroit, Chicago, and Philadelphia. This put pressure on resources such as housing and increased competition for jobs. And this pressure led to tension between the new arrivals and those who were fighting for their livelihoods. Segregation in housing was declared illegal, but landlords would use other methods to keep their properties out of the hands of certain groups. Racial tension was particularly high in Chicago, and this turned to tragedy in 1919 when a Black man drowned following an attack by several white men. When the police refused to arrest the attackers, a week of riots between white and Black gangs, leading to 38 deaths and numerous injuries, not to mention over 1000 burned homes.

Given the range of measures preventing Blacks and other minorities from being treated as "equal" despite the Declaration of Independence and adding the violence they were subjected to post-Civil War, it is probably not surprising that the minorities started fighting back. Civil rights protests and organized demonstrations would result in segregation being outlawed, but changing laws is not the same as changing attitudes.

Do PoC commit more crimes? Statistically, yes. In the US, Blacks make up about 13% of the population, but FBI figures confirm that they commit about 27% of all crimes. Native Americans make up about 2% of the population, and this roughly correlates to the percentages of crimes they commit (2.4%). Is race a factor in high crime rates? Not likely. Too many other factors, particularly poverty, are more plausible reasons for the high crime rate among PoC.

But anger and resentment caused by decades of unfair or brutal treatment could also be behind the high crime stats. The gang life has its appeal among those who feel that society has let them down. Children whose parents have been sent to prison will have grown up without a stabilizing influence or been raised in the foster system. Drugs and alcohol abuse are major factors in many crimes.

As they tend to be less well-off, the PoC faces another disadvantage when it comes to being arrested for crimes. And that is that they are less likely to be able to afford the best lawyers. A good lawyer will know all the best tips and tricks to get their client off, and if this fails, then to have the sentence as minimal as possible. We already mentioned the cases where wealthy people managed to get short sentences for crimes such as rape (three months). A court-appointed lawyer will also have a range of clients on their docket, so they would more likely be stretched for time. They may have the ability and the qualifications to do their best for their clients, but they may not have the time.

Black people are far more likely to be arrested for drug offenses than any other group. They are also more likely to serve longer sentences for similar crimes. A 2017 report by the United States Sentencing Commission shows that sentences are approximately 19% longer for Black males than for any other group. This report adjusted the statistics to take into account any prior convictions the person might have.

Many states in the US also adopt a "three strikes" rule, in which a person who is considered to be a habitual offender can land out with a life sentence for what would normally be considered a petty crime. Fair Wayne Bryant of Louisiana served 23 years for stealing a set of hedge clippers. Anthony Jackson of South Carolina received a life sentence for stealing a wallet and using a stolen credit card. An American Civil Liberties Union (ACLU) report in 2013 found over 3,000 people were serving life sentences for trivial crimes. These include:

- possession of a crack pipe
- possession of 32 grams of marijuana with intent to distribute
- acting as a go-between in the sale of $10 of marijuana to an undercover officer
- sharing several grams of LSD with Grateful Dead concertgoers
- having a stash of over-the-counter decongestant pills that could be manufactured into methamphetamine
- possession of a bottle cap containing a trace, unweighable amount of heroin
- having a trace amount of cocaine in clothes pockets that was so minute it was invisible to the naked eye and detected only in lab tests

- having a single, small crack rock at home
- attempting to cash a stolen check
- a junk dealer's possession of stolen junk metal (10 valves and one elbow pipe)
- possession of stolen wrenches
- making a drunken threat to a police officer while handcuffed in the back of a patrol car

In 1991, Rodney King was drunk and in charge of a vehicle. Several Los Angeles police officers pursued and arrested him. So far, so good. What happened next, not so much. In the days before cell phones, someone still managed to video the brutal beating King got from the four police officers. And when those four officers were acquitted of using excessive force against King, LA erupted into violence. A combination of anger against the perceived unfairness of the verdict and anger over the beating itself, coupled with years of racial tension and complaints that the LAPD were racially profiling Blacks, resulted in six days of chaos, over 60 deaths, and an estimated $1 billion in damages.

And are Black and other minorities actually committing the crimes they are accused of? Racial profiling is rife, according to studies by the ACLU. Official information has demonstrated that Black people are three times as likely to be stopped and searched[1] in routine traffic stops. Traffic stops are often used not to investigate driving offenses but suspicions of other crimes, such as drug trafficking. When looking for crime suspects, the police target the poorer neighborhoods, as odds are the criminal is from there. Give the lower socioeconomic status of many PoC in the USA. It's fair to say that the police are also targeting Black, Hispanic, or other minorities when going into these neighborhoods.

Police can argue that given it is statistically more likely that a PoC is responsible for a crime, that they are using the laws of probability when searching for suspects, not unconscious bias. However, this is a bit of a "chicken and egg" problem. Yes, Black people feature heavily in crime stats, technically justifying the police then assuming that a Black person is responsible for this particular crime. But if the Black person is angry about unfair or racist treatment and feels frustrated because of other, non-criminal but still debilitating circumstances, and this drives them to crime, how much of a role did the assumption that "Black = criminal" play in this?

Then there are the crimes committed against PoC that would not, in all likelihood, be committed against non-PoC. Police shootings feature heavily here, but civilians must take their share of responsibility for their own bias. Ahmaud Abery was jogging. George Floyd was being detained (without resisting) by police. Breanna Taylor, Atatiana Jefferson, Botham Jean, and Kathryn Johnson were all at home (in Taylor's case, she was asleep). Tamir Rice was playing with a toy. Trayvon Martin was carrying a pack of candy. Sandra Bland got a traffic ticket. Walter Scott was running away from the police. Philando Castile was legally carrying a weapon. Jordan Davis was playing loud music. After 9/11, anyone who looked Muslim also became the target of attacks (even if they were not Muslim, such as the unfortunate Sikh Balbir Singh Sodhi, mentioned in the last chapter).

Given the decades of abuse and prejudice and the indication that PoC are more likely to be accused of and convicted of crimes, it is hardly surprising that whole communities might have a distrust of the police or the legal system. And with that in mind, the likelihood of a PoC using preventative measures to curb crime, such as early intervention for troubled children, is small.

Much of the focus of this chapter has been on whether PoC are committing more crimes (they are) and whether they are treated less fairly (they are) in the USA. However, the USA is not unique. At the start, we talked about Canada, Australia, and New Zealand (all with a predominantly Caucasian population) as having similarly high incarceration rates among the indigenous (not quite as Caucasian) population. And in New Zealand, in the 1970s, a ridiculous case of color-blindness demonstrated the disparity between what a white person can get away with, crime-wise, versus a non-white person.

During the 1970s, police in New Zealand were helping to crack down on illegal immigrants, particularly those from Pacific countries. As a result, many people with a Pacifica appearance or name were often pulled up by police and asked to account for themselves. One such case was when a young man from Niue was stopped while walking home from work and asked to show his work visa. As he was from Niue (a protectorate of New Zealand) he wasn't required to hold a work visa—he was in the country legally. However, he was carrying three combs, taken from his employer (a firm that manufactured them). The police officer who pulled him up asked him about these combs, and when he said that he had taken them from his employer, he was arrested for theft. Each comb was valued at approximately 20 cents, and it was common practice (and one encouraged by the employer) to take these from the reject bin. Had the police contacted the man's employer, they would have found this out.

When a law lecturer heard about this, he took a pen from his employer, the University of Auckland. The value of the pen was also about 20 cents. He took the pen home, then went to the police and told them what he had done. The police asked him whether he was working at home (in which case his "theft" would have been justified). He denied this. The police then offered to call his employer, something they didn't do for the young Niuean. The law lecturer pointed out that he had stolen the pen and should be arrested. The police refused to do so because when they called his employer, the employer refused to press charges. Unsurprisingly, the law lecturer was white.

A person of color starts life with the disadvantage that prejudice brings. Add that to the likelihood of having been raised under less than salubrious circumstances and the lack of faith in the justice system, and suddenly a perfect storm is created. If people of color commit more crimes than any other racial group, is it really that strange?

CHAPTER 10
CRIME AND PUNISHMENT

"To have once been a criminal is no disgrace. To remain a criminal is the disgrace." ~ Malcolm X

Having spent the bulk of this book on the topic of criminals and what makes them the way they are, it is time to think about the consequences of any criminal act. On the perpetrator, on the victims, on the families, and on society in general. Crime never occurs in a vacuum.

For the perpetrator, the consequences of their crimes vary. The final act of any criminal case is sentencing. For petty crimes, this could be a formal warning, a fine, a period on probation, or community service. If you have seen "volunteers" cleaning up trash from the side of the road, they could be doing so as part of a deal over a petty crime—do some public service and avoid jail time or a fine. A criminal may be ordered to pay damages to their victims. A drunk driver might lose their license or gain demerit points. Home detention is a possibility, where the criminal is required to stay confined to their home, usually with a monitoring bracelet on so that if they step out of the approved designated area (without permission), they trigger an alarm. They may be asked to take part in a restorative justice program in which they meet their victims and listen to how the crime affected them. This, presumably, is to make the criminal aware of the consequences of their actions and to ram home the suggestion that there are no victimless crimes—every crime has consequences. Putting a human face to the criminal act may help the criminal develop empathy for their victim. If the criminal committed a crime under the influence of drugs or alcohol, attending a rehab program might also form part of their sentence. First-time sex offenders (assuming the crime they committed is of a minor enough nature, such as obscene exposure) might be allowed to partake in therapy sessions to help them deal with these urges. All of these measures are put in place to help the criminal understand that they have committed harm, but at the same time, allows a chance for redemption.

As the crime becomes more serious, so too do the punishments, with the first step being short-term incarceration. As its name implies, the person committing the crime is sent to a detention facility. In theory, this removes the criminal from society, thereby protecting society from any further criminal acts by that person. It also acts as a deterrent because who wants to spend time in jail, away from home comforts, family, and freedom? So surely, if a criminal is sent to jail, they are unlikely to re-offend because they know how bad things can get. Jail time always works, after all. And anyone who knows the criminal will be put off by the fact that they have been sent to jail.

In practice? In practice, sending people to prison for a short time will, naturally, expose them to other criminals. Few people go to prison and spend their time in isolation. We already talked about the effect our peers have on our behavior and how being part of the group influences us. So when we are in prison, surrounded by fellow criminals, it would hardly be surprising that we take the tone of the company we keep.

A combination of longer sentences and the rise of incarceration for what would once be considered misdemeanors has resulted in an increase in custodial sentences. This can be put down to a combination of issues around sentencing. A petty criminal may receive a sentence that includes payment of a fine or restitution, but if they are unable to afford to pay that fine, the alternative is to serve time. If the judge has ordered asset forfeiture as part of the sentence, that adds to the criminal's financial burden (seizure of a car, for instance, may mean that the criminal can no longer get to work). If probation or home detention is not feasible, the alternative is prison. And jail as a deterrent to other would-be criminals clearly doesn't work because the prison population is growing, not shrinking. And the longer sentence times, especially in relation to the "three strikes" law, keeps people in prison who might otherwise have been released.

Prisons mainly offer the option for rehab programs while the criminal is still serving time. This includes programs such as anger management and focuses on reinforcing positive behaviors rather than punishing bad behaviors. They usually include therapy for drug and alcohol dependency, and many programs offer vocational advice as well to improve the criminal's chance of coping once released.

These programs are particularly important when it comes to sex offenders. Before being released, most sex offenders generally must have attended therapy sessions to reduce the likelihood of them re-offending.

The benefits of rehab programs, particularly for lower-end offenses, have been demonstrated to work. Not in every case, of course, and rehab is usually not an option in more serious cases. But various studies, including one by the American Psychological Association in 2004, shows that rehabilitation, particularly drug rehabilitation, reduces recidivism—in the APA study, only 27% of those who went through drug rehabilitation returned to prison. Other studies conducted by the National Institute of Justice estimate that recidivism could reduce by approximately 15%–20% if rehabilitation programs were extended.

If the criminal is fortunate enough to be released after only a few months, they face other challenges. We talked about these in Chapter Three, when we mentioned the difficulties a convicted criminal faces when it comes to finding employment. They have also been estranged from family and support networks (albeit for a short time), and these can take time to repair. There may be some rehab programs that the released prisoner can take part in, but how effective these programs are, depends on whether there are sufficient resources to make the program worthwhile. And it also depends on the willingness of the criminal to engage.

If they are released on probation, they will have conditions imposed on them as part of their probation, such as avoiding criminal contacts, attending drug or alcohol programs, and restrictions on where they can live. Some criminals are banned from using the internet (particularly when they have committed crimes such as cybercrime or were convicted of stalking or harassment online). Work release programs are designed to make it easier for the criminal to find work despite having a record. These are all part of making sure that the criminal doesn't, or at least is less likely to, re-offend. Rehabilitation into society after a short time out of it is feasible, depending on the resources available to run these programs as well as the criminal's willingness to participate.

The longer a criminal is behind bars, the less likely they are to reintegrate. Their job opportunities are few, even allowing for the fact that their employable skills will have become rusty while inside. Suppose an employer is offered a choice between two equally qualified candidates, and one has a prison record, especially for violent crime or robbery. In that case, it's only to be expected that the employer chooses the one who hasn't served time. Spouses may have moved on, and children will have grown older without the input of the absent parent. Elderly parents may have died.

The only time when a criminal is almost guaranteed to die behind bars is when sentenced to extremely long sentences (for example, life + 300 years) or sentenced to death. In the USA, 27 states have the death penalty, and this is most often imposed for murder only. It is, however, available for other crimes such as treason, aggravated kidnapping, and large-scale drug trafficking. Whether these most extreme of sentences act as a deterrent to would-be criminals is debatable. Murder is so often committed in the heat of the moment, such as a violent assault, that it is hard to argue the murderer really thought about the possibility of incarceration or the prospect of a death sentence before committing that murder.

Even in cases of premeditated murder, the murderer is in all likelihood considering all the ways not to be caught, not so much because of the fear of having to face the needle, but because of the belief that they can get away with murder if they plan convincingly. We talked about some murderers in earlier chapters. Ian Brady and Myra Hindley were both committing their crimes at a time when the death penalty was still the penalty for murder in the UK. It didn't stop them from murdering child after child. Rose and Fred West murdered children and young women partly out of their warped sexual fantasies but also to ensure their safety (silencing those who posed a threat). John Wayne Gacy was executed, but there was little in his pattern of offending that indicated he was afraid of being caught. Was Dennis Rader? Charles Manson? Eric Harris and Dylan Klebold both opted for suicide, so it's unlikely that they would have worried about the death penalty—they might even have welcomed it. Leopold and Loeb were arrogant enough to believe they could commit murder and get away with it, as did Michael Skakel.

The United States has one of the highest rates of recidivism in the world, with an estimated 44% of criminals being reconvicted within a year of release. Breaking the cycle of recidivism is something that would benefit both the criminal and those who would normally be victims.

Reducing crime numbers will obviously reduce the number of people who are on the receiving end of crime. Who wants to be robbed or attacked? Despite what some might say, no one asks to be raped. Certainly, no one asks to be murdered. We should have the right to walk the streets without fear of being assaulted, to drive to our destination without being involved in a crash with a drunk driver, and to come home to find our possessions intact. We send our children to school, fully expecting that they will come home. If we build up a company, we don't expect our employees to hack our accounts and embezzle. Even the so-called "victimless" crimes—recreational drug use, gambling, assisted suicide, public drunkenness, and prostitution (depending on region)—can have a negative effect on the person committing that "crime."

We talked about the rehabilitation of the criminal as being a way of ending the cycle of crime, but there are vocal groups who believe that nothing works, that more care is given to the criminal than the victim, and they should all be strung up anyway. This is especially so when the crime is violent, or the victim is vulnerable. Thanks to the rise of social media and commenting forums, it is easy to rouse anger against the criminal. But victims are often forgotten in a rush to condemn the criminal. How many times is it said of rapists that "hope they get raped in jail." Ironic, really, because doesn't that then make them rape victims?

Anyone can be the victim of a crime, as we mentioned in the first chapter. And the most common victim, particularly of violent crime, is related to the perpetrator. The tragedy then multiplies. If a female is killed by her spouse (one of the most common examples of murder), then not only is she dead, but if there are any children involved, they have lost their mother and their father or stepfather. Their family unit is broken. It is unlikely that the murder of their mother was the only time they witnessed violence in the home. The kids are traumatized, and now they are probably having to go into the care of family members, or worse, the foster system. There is nothing inherently wrong with the foster system, but it doesn't necessarily make for a stable upbringing for the children. How much damage has the murderer inflicted on their victim's families, as well as their victim?

The rape victim must cope with the aftermath of the attack. This includes reporting the crime and having to go through a physical examination. Always assuming that they report the crime—as mentioned, rape is one of the most unreported crimes. Then there's the trial (if the case is prosecuted). The victim has to relive the crime and face their attacker. If the defense attorney is doing their job, they will attack the victim in an effort to make their story less believable. Rebuilding relationships with partners after rape can be problematic.

Anyone who has ever been burgled will know that the burglary is just the start of the problem. Immediate replacement of urgent items has to be a priority, but as anyone who has to buy in a hurry will already know, the first-choice items may not be available or at a reasonable price. If your car is stolen, there goes your means of transport, and now you are dependent on others, or public transport. Insurance claims take time to process, and it's unlikely you will get what you consider to be a fair replacement price. And no amount of money can take away the psychological trauma of being burgled—the loss of personal security, the theft or damage of items of sentimental value that can never be replaced.

A business that has lost money thanks to the fraud of an employee may well go bankrupt. The bank teller who had to hand the money over to a gun-toting robber still has to front up to work and potentially relive the trauma of looking at a loaded gun. The person who was beaten up has physical as well as mental injuries. They have to go through medical procedures to fix broken bones and damaged limbs and will probably need time off work, leading to more issues with their employers, who may be unsympathetic to their employee's needs. Mental injuries are not always covered by insurance, so any counseling is done at the victim's expense.

Society's reaction to increasing crime is usually to demand tougher sentences and more police power. The more crime-ridden the area is, the angrier people get, and when people get angry, they lose the ability to think rationally or even compassionately. We demand the book be thrown at criminals who might otherwise have been rehabilitated. We demand more money for law and order, and as soon as this happens, there is less money for beneficial causes. We shudder at the thought of investing in programs to help criminals reintegrate because why should they get the money? They committed the crime, and they can damn well do the time. If you don't want to live like a crim, stop acting like one.

Whatever we think about our police force, we tend to expect a high standard of professionalism from them. They are there to protect us, but as has been widely demonstrated in cases where police actions were doubtful, corrupt, or straight-up murderous, not all police adhere to those high standards. And when they fail, we lose faith in them, so we don't report a crime or request appropriate intervention when crimes are being committed. Vigilante rule is not the way to go—we are just replacing one set of criminals with another.

Certain criminals must be punished. They must be locked up for everyone's safety and to help in the healing of their victims. But it shouldn't be necessary in all cases and investing in rehab programs is a far better way of protecting society, victims, and families than punitive sentences.

CONCLUSION

If it's inevitable, what can we do to stop it?

We have a few choices when it comes to crime. We can pretend it doesn't exist. That's fairly easy for most of us, seeing we are probably not the victims nor the perpetrator. We merely read about it, tsk at how society has degraded, and move on to the next story (probably also a crime story).

But just because we're not affected by crime doesn't mean that in some way, we haven't contributed to it. We didn't force the young solo mother to have a baby, thereby putting that child into a family environment that possibly (not inevitably) was less than healthy, but at some stage, we agreed that birth control laws should be tightened and the criteria for welfare payments and social housing be closely examined. We might not be actively racist, but did we look at the person who was following us (who might have just been walking home) and wondered… and having wondered, thought about calling the police? What about looking the other way when we see bullying? We are not all guilty of crimes, nor should we hold collective guilt over crimes in which we had no involvement. But we should always be conscious that our actions might have consequences. After all, we expect criminals to grasp this basic fact!

So, when it comes to crime, what can we do?

There is no quick fix, but let's consider a few ideas. As we identified eight causes, let's think about eight possible solutions.

1. Addressing the family issues. If we know of cases where there are children raised in abusive situations, speak up, or provide support to those who want to get out of those situations. As a way to solve family problems, this is far more likely to work than if we simply judge those who make what we consider to be poor choices.

2. Plan and prepare, where possible, for any downturns in financial status. Anyone can lose a job. If we are fortunate enough to have enough money, actively support groups that help the poor, rather than just assuming that "lazy bludgers" are going to spend their government assistance on drugs and booze.

3. Talk to our children about drugs and alcohol. If we are affected by addiction, don't be afraid to seek help. We can do this in confidence.

4. If we see or hear of bullying, at school, in the community, and in the workplace—speak up. Bullies almost never act without support.

5. Hold our politicians and public figures to account. Voting is a tool that is available (although, ironically, not to criminals),

but voter turnout in elections is often staggeringly low. Even between elections, speak up when we hear politicians trying to incite violence against a particular group.

6. Give the same respect to other people's religions and beliefs that we would expect them to show to ours. There are literally thousands of religions in the world—if mine is right, then those 9,999 or so others are wrong. Is that even logical?

7. Don't let joblessness get us down. This is a toughie, but volunteer work, involving ourselves in the community, and using networks are all handy ways to keep yourself busy during downtimes.

8. Speak up, loudly and clearly, when we see or hear of racism, and avoid stereotyping based on race, religion, sexual orientation, or belief.

It's important to realize that any of us can become criminals if our circumstances change and for many of us, it's sheer luck that we are not. Remember how we talked about the birth lottery? There but for the grace of God go I, or some other bringing-down-to-earth belief like walking in another person's shoes to understand why and how they are like they are can help us to see criminals for what they (mostly) are—us, with a bit of bad luck thrown in the mix. And understanding that might help us to understand how we can work with criminals to reduce their likelihood of re-offending.

If this book speaks to you, please share it with others—criminals or otherwise.

ABOUT THE AUTHOR

Hi, I'm Marley Hill, a New Zealand based author. I'm a writer who goes to the nth degree to research my subject, to inform and educate my audience. I'm well-travelled, I have a public health related background and have seen personally, the consequences of what life choices can have on society.

My passions – writing and my desire for privacy. I have written many articles, and a few years ago, a couple of short books, I really love to write. It's what I do in my spare time; it's how I relax. It's the job that doesn't feel like a job.

The research involved in writing my books, the need to cite sources carefully and accurately, and the need to maintain a neutral position are all skills that I pride myself in. My opinions don't count, but my presentation of the facts do.

REFERENCES

CHAPTER 1

1) Office of Justice Programs Statistical Briefing Book. Retrieved from https://www.ojjdp.gov/ojstatbb/crime/ucr.asp?table_in=1&selYrs=2019&rdoGroups=1&rdoData=c

2) FBI – 2016 Crimes in the United States. Retrieved from https://ucr.fbi.gov/crime-in-the-u.s/2016/crime-in-the-u.s.-2016/tables/table-20

3) Ranking of the most dangerous cities in the world. Retrieved from https://www.statista.com/statistics/243797/ranking-of-the-most-dangerous-cities-in-the-world-by-murder-rate-per-capita/

4) RAINN Perpetrators of Sexual violence. Retrieved from https://www.rainn.org/statistics/perpetrators-sexual-violence

5) Recidivism of adult felons. Retrieved from https://www.cfc.wa.gov/PublicationSentencing/Recidivism/Adult_Recidivism_FY2007.pdf

CHAPTER 2

1) Long-term consequences of child abuse and neglect. Retrieved from https://www.childwelfare.gov/pubpdfs/long_term_consequences.pdf

2) The Effect of Adverse Childhood Experience on Clinical Diagnosis of a Substance Use Disorder: Results of a Nationally Representative Study. Retrieved from https://pubmed.ncbi.nlm.nih.gov/28145794/

3) McLeod, S. A. (2016, February 05). *Bandura - social learning theory*. Simply Psychology. Retrieved from https://www.simplypsychology.org/bandura.html

4) Researchers study intergenerational transmission of criminal behavior. Retrieved from https://phys.org/news/2017-11-children-criminal-parents-greater-chance.html

CHAPTER 4

1) Impaired driving – get the facts. Retrieved from https://www.cdc.gov/transportationsafety/impaired_driving/impaired-drv_factsheet.html#:~:text=In%202016%2C%2010%2C497%20people%20died,deaths%20in%20the%20United%20States.&text=Of%20the%201%2C233%20traffic%20deaths,involved%20an%20alcohol%2Dimpaired%20driver

2) Alcohol-related crimes. Retrieved from
   https://www.alcoholrehabguide.org/alcohol/crimes/

CHAPTER 5

1) Violence among teens can spread like a disease. Retrieved from
   https://www.smithsonianmag.com/science-nature/teenagers-violent-friends-are-more-likely-be-violent-themselves-180961526/

2) About violent gangs. Retrieved from
   https://www.justice.gov/criminal-ocgs/about-violent-gangs

3) Gang statistics. Retrieved from
   https://www.justice.gov/archives/jm/criminal-resource-manual-103-gang-statistics

4) National Gang Threat Assessment – Emerging Trends. Retrieved from https://www.fbi.gov/file-repository/stats-services-publications-2011-national-gang-threat-assessment-2011%20national%20gang%20threat%20assessment%20%20emerging%20trends.pdf/view

CHAPTER 6

1) Conflict management and Peace Science. Retrieved from
https://journals.sagepub.com/doi/full/10.1177/0738894216661190

CHAPTER 7

1) A brief history of the Salem Witch Trials. Retrieved from https://www.smithsonianmag.com/history/a-brief-history-of-the-salem-witch-trials-175162489/

CHAPTER 9

1) Study indicates racial profiling by Oakland cops. Retrieved from https://www.sfgate.com/bayarea/article/Study-indicates-racial-profiling-by-Oakland-cops-2921498.php

Made in United States
Troutdale, OR
07/07/2023